# Paris

## Select

# contents

# Paris overview

Capital of romance, of fashion, of food, of intellectuals and philosophers, famed for its historic buildings and monuments and for that indefinable *je ne sais quoi* that makes up French chic, Paris is a city that likes to live up to its myths; but it is also a modern working city, of financial institutions, of scientific discoveries and learned research institutes.

Don't be fooled into thinking of Paris as a museum. Paris has always modernised, over the centuries expanding in concentric circles outwards from the Ile de la Cité, and has never been afraid to drop in radical new monuments or reinvent old ones. On the one hand you can find Roman baths sticking up in the middle of a Gothic mansion, on the other the glass pyramid at the Louvre and a shiny white UFO by Zaha Hadid that has just landed at the Institut du Monde Arabe. Two of the most recent cultural venues occupy both a converted theatre and a former undertaker's, new parks have been created around the city's edges, and an entire new district is taking root above old railway sidings around the new Bibliothèque Nationale, along the Seine.

If there is one recommended requisite to making the most of the city, it is curiosity. This is a place where you come to admire the grand facades and imperious vistas, the world-renowned museums and glorious churches – but must also be everready to peer through carriage doorways or wander down passageways to discover the hidden gardens, concealed houses and workshops that make up the private, intimate Paris behind the bravura. One of the most appealing aspects of the city is that it is intensely lived in. Part of the fun of wandering round the streets is discovering the local street market, the favourite spot for a coffee and the best baker. Residents continue to privilege what they call the 'style de vie' – lifestyle – which means that for all the apparent rush, there is always time to stroll around the food market or sit at a café terrace for coffee or an aperitif.

# in the mood for...

## ... gastronomy

Evidence of the Parisians' love of food can be seen everywhere from street markets and busy lunchtime cafés to grand dining establishments. While the image relayed abroad is often of elitist grand dining involving squadrons of waiters and silver cloches – recently awarded Unesco heritage status – and once-in-a-lifetime meals in the sumptuous surroundings of **Le Meurice** *(p.50)*, **Le Grand Véfour** *(p.49)* or **Pierre Gagnaire** *(p.71)*, the reality is much more varied and depends on your mood or budget. The mainstay are bistros and brasseries, trad places such as **Bistrot Paul Bert** *(p.105)*, **La Fontaine de Mars** *(p.143)*, or budget institution **Chartier** *(p.61)*. However many bistros are renewing the genre, mixing tradition with modern seasonal dishes at **Astier** *(p.105)*, **Mon Vieil Ami** *(p.30)*, 'bistronomiques' like **Chez L'Ami Jean** *(p.143)*, Christian Constant's chic diner **Les Cocottes** *(p.143)*, or **Playtime** *(p.94)* with its fusion touches – always with an emphasis on quality ingredients but retaining the informal mood and reasonable prices.

## ... romance

Paris enjoys an image as one of the world's most romantic cities, yet what makes it romantic is hard to pin down. Rather, it all comes down to an endless collection of the smallest things: misty early morning views of the quais of **Ile St-Louis** *(p.30)*, the glamour of watching opera or ballet ensconced in red satin and velvet in a box at **Palais Garnier** *(p.56)*, relaxing in the beautiful, intimate square that is **place des Vosges** *(p.32)* with its red brick arcades, being lushly immersed in foliage in the steamy **Serres d'Auteuil** *(p.55)* hot houses, the timeless charm of a stroll along the **Canal St-Martin** *(p.102)* or the pathos of the **cemetery at Montmartre** *(p.87)*. Then again, romance might come in the shape of a grand summer meal for two under a parasol in the gardens at **Laurent** *(p.71)*, or as a memorable stay in a fine hotel – in a sweeping terrace suite at the **Shangri-La Paris** *(p.171)*, where the Eiffel Tower seems almost close enough to touch perhaps, or the indulgence of beams and luscious fabrics at the **Hôtel du Petit Moulin** *(p.40)*.

## ... retail therapy

Paris lives up to its reputation as a fashion capital with the couture houses of **avenue Montaigne** (*p.70*) and cutting-edge cuts at **Palais-Royal** (*p.49*). Those who want to keep track of trends follow groundbreaking concept store **Colette** (*p.53*) and its alter ego **Merci** (*p.41*). And while the *grands magasins (pictured, p.62)* offer an awe-inspiring choice, the charm of Paris shopping lies in the city's boutiques: say **Shine** or **Swildens** in the Haut-Marais (*p.40*), or kitchen emporium **E Dehellerin** (*p.55*), an endearing relic of the Les Halles market.

## ... observing Parisians

What could be more Parisian than watching Parisians? Parisians excel at it, sitting on café terraces to see and be seen. Maybe that's what café society is all about: spotting famous faces at **Café de Flore** and **Les Deux Magots** (*p.123*), sizing up the fashion brigade at **L'Avenue** (*p.70*), inspecting other people's purchases at **Café Charlot** (*p.41*). Catch the diversity of streetlife at **Marché d'Aligre** (*p.101*) or **Abbesses** (*p.85*), children and charmers in the **Jardin du Luxembourg** (*p.125*), smart families in **Parc Monceau** (*p.76*), and trendies at **Chez Jeannette** (*p.94*).

## ... a view

Remember that Paris once boasted the tallest building in the world – the **Eiffel Tower** *(p.138)* – and you'll realise that there are plenty of things to climb here: the steep tower of **Notre-Dame Cathedral** *(p.26)*, the gazebo in **Parc des Buttes-Chaumont** *(p.104)*, the dome of the **Panthéon** *(p.118)*. Some of the best views are the panoramas afforded by the city's hills – from the top of the steps leading up to the **Sacré-Coeur** *(pictured, p.90)*, zooming into the city centre from the **Parc de Belleville** *(p.106)*, across the Seine from the **Domaine de St-Cloud** *(p.166)*. Perfect vantage points are often to be found not too high up but at roof level: ideal for glimpses of private lives in apartments and secret roof gardens; try the summer rooftop restaurants at **Galeries Lafayette** and **Printemps** *(p.62)*, or the escalator ride up the **Centre Pompidou** *(p.34)*, where the city spreads out before you as you rise and you can dine with a view at Georges.

## ... family fun

Paris is a family-friendly city awash with parks and climbing frames and those with kids have a great excuse to go up the **Eiffel Tower** *(p.138)*. The **Jardin des Plantes** *(pictured, p.114)* is good for all ages with the Ménagerie and brilliantly displayed Grande Galerie de l'Evolution. There are special children's sections at the **Cité des Sciences** *(p.156)* and fun playgrounds outside. Bigger kids get a thrill from the prison cells at the **Conciergerie** *(p.28)*, macabre bones at **Les Catacombes** *(p.145)* or vintage flying machines at the **Musée des Arts et Métiers** *(p.43)*. Don't be intimidated by the size of the large museums: the **Centre Pompidou** *(p.34)* has specially conceived exhibitions in its Galerie des Enfants, there are Impressionists galore at **Musée d'Orsay** *(p.134)*, and all the Egyptian mummies a child could desire at the **Louvre** *(p.48)*. This is also a good city for eating out with kids – do as the Parisians do. Go for bustle and spectacle at **La Coupôle** brasserie *(p.144)*, friendly **Astier** *(p.105)* or budget legend **Chartier** *(p.61)*, for watching the waiter memorise the orders.

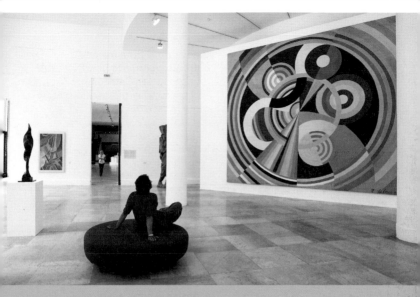

### ... fine art

The **Louvre** *(p.48)* is the super museum to beat all museums, the **Centre Pompidou** *(p.34)* feels like a voyage through modern art, and there are also major temporary exhibitions on show at the **Grand Palais** *(p.68)* and the **Musée d'Art Moderne de la Ville de Paris** *(pictured, p.74)*. For contemporary art, see what's happening at the **Palais de Tokyo** *(p.74)*, or hit the preview circuit at the **Marais private galleries** *(p.31)* and the new galleries colonising **Belleville** *(p.106)*. Impressionism was perhaps the Parisian art movement par excellence, and superb collections are to be found at **Musée d'Orsay** *(p.134)*, **Musée Marmottan Monet** *(p.152)* and the **Orangerie** *(p.54)*. Individual collectors have made their mark at **Musée Jaquemart-André** *(p.72)*, with gems of the Italian Renaissance, or Dina Vierny's **Musée Maillol** *(p.140)*, while houses and studios impart a personal insight into the life of the artist at the eccentric **Musée Gustave Moreau** *(p.86)*, the atmosphere of an old Montparnasse artist's studio at **Musée Bourdelle** *(p.147)* or the sheer virtuosity and creativity of Auguste Rodin at **Musée Rodin** *(p.137)*.

## ... multicultural Paris

Paris has always drawn in migrants but probably never more so than today, a history traced at the **Cité de l'Immigration** *(p.160)*. The tower blocks of **Chinatown** *(p.161)* harbour Chinese restaurants and exotic supermarkets, Little Japan flourishes on **rue Ste-Anne** *(p.63)*, and Middle Europe meets North Africa in the Jewish food shops on **rue des Rosiers** *(pictured, p.36)*. Wander along **Faubourg-St-Denis** *(p.94)*, where a bar scene is developing amid ethnic grocers and Indian restaurants, and discover multicultural comic talent at **Le Comedy Club** *(p.57)*.

## ... outdoor lazing

In intensely lived in, densely populated Paris, where most Parisians are starved of gardens, the city does its best to make up for it with a panoply of squares, parks and playgrounds. Even in the city centre the pace slows down in tranquil, hidden spots like the **Arènes de Lutèce** *(p.119)*, while the **Jardin du Luxembourg** *(pictured, p.125)* is just made for surveying the scene – lazily – from a Luxembourg chair. Paris is great for walking. Amble along the **Canal St-Martin** *(p.102)* on a Sunday, to pause at canalside cafés or watch as barges chug through the locks.

## ... historic journeys

It can feel as if you are totally surrounded by history in Paris, simply by the airy beauty of **Eglise St-Etienne-du-Mont** (*p.128*), the golden facades of the **Marais mansions** (*p.31*) or the unbelievable number of writers, politicians, generals, artists, singers and inventors who shaped the city resting in **Père Lachaise cemetery** (*p.108*) or of great men honoured at the **Panthéon** (*pictured, p.118*). There are traces of medieval and Roman Paris at the **Musée National du Moyen-Age** (*p.116*), royal tombs at **St-Denis** (*p.165*), royal residences at the **Château de Vincennes** (*p.167*) and the **Louvre** (*p.48*), and

Napoleon at **Les Invalides** (*p.136*). The Revolution of 1789 meanwhile is powerfully evoked in the prison cells of the **Conciergerie** (*p.28*), and by the solitude of the **Chapelle Expiatoire** (*p.77*) and **Cimetière de Picpus** (*p.100*). Some things seem to have barely changed in centuries: the timewarped 17th-century perfection of **Ile St-Louis** (*p.30*), the house of a mythic *Merveilleuse* at the **Petit Hôtel Bourrienne** (*p.95*) – where Fortunée Hamelin entertained visitors from her bath, its gorgeous decor intact – or the incredible craftsmanship on view at the **Manufacture des Gobelins** (*p.120*), a working historic factory.

## ... literary inspiration

Paris kicks off the September start of term with an outpouring of new books, and you'll still find writers today in the traditional publishing heartland of St-Germain, following Sartre and de Beauvoir to **Café de Flore** *(p.123)*. Hemingway and Orwell found literary inspiration – and cheap meals – around **place de la Contrescarpe** *(p.121)* and you can sit at the same table as the former at **La Closerie des Lilas** *(p.144)*. Discover souvenirs of Marcel Proust at **Musée Carnavalet** *(p.33)*, **Victor Hugo's apartment** *(p.32)*, and **George Sand**'s affair with Chopin *(p.88)*.

## ... a night out

Numerous bars and brasseries around town stay open until 1 or 2am. Arty young hipsters flock to the Canal St-Martin or Faubourg-St-Denis, while St-Germain has a more classic cocktail scene. Good rock venues include the **Trianon** and **La Cigale** in Pigalle *(p.91)*, while live music and clubbing thrives at **Batofar** *(p.126)* as well as in other boats cum floating venues on the Seine, free from the noise restrictions of many districts. One of Paris's most surprising night spots is also on – or in– the river: **Showcase** *(p.69)*, hidden inside the Pont Alexandre III bridge.

## ... modern architecture

Most people associate Paris with historic heritage, yet the city has never been afraid to inject the urban fabric with radical new buildings that initially shocked but have now been adopted, such as Rogers and Piano's exciting coloured tubes at the **Centre Pompidou** *(p.34)* and I M Pei's glass **Pyramid** at the Louvre *(p.48)*, joined more recently by the baroque form of Jean Nouvel's **Musée du Quai Branly** *(pictured, p.141)*. Fans of the Modern Movement should head to the **Fondation Le Corbusier** *(p.153)* and the **Cité Universitaire** *(p.153)*. Catch an overview of modern architecture at the **Cité de l'Architecture** *(p.73)* and see a whole district in the making, growing up around the **Bibliothèque Nationale François Mitterrand** *(p.126)*. Meanwhile, the **Institut du Monde Arabe** *(p.129)* is a rare chance to see two buildings by Pritzker prizewinning architects, Jean Nouvel and Zaha Hadid, side by side.

## ... village life

Paris is often described as a collection of villages, each with its distinctive character and style, and many Parisians are intensely attached to their *quartier*. Some of these neighbourhoods were once bona fide villages, for instance **Charonne** *(p.159)*, **Batignolles** *(p.93)* and hilly **Montmartre** *(pictured, p.84)*. Elsewhere it's a question of mood, a picturesque enclave such as **Quartier Mouzaïa** *(p.104)*, the alleyways of **Faubourg-St-Antoine** *(p.107)* colonised by artists and designers, or the charm of the **Mouffetard district** *(p.121)*, with its much-loved markets.

## ... science and technology

Paris's scientific heritage is often overlooked, yet the marks of engineering prowess are stamped all over the ironwork of the **Eiffel Tower** *(p.138)* and the nave of the **Grand Palais** *(p.68)*, as well as unseen and underground in **Les Egouts** *(p.146)*, keeping the city functioning today. There are excellent science and technology collections at the **Cité des Sciences** *(pictured, p.156)* and the **Musée des Arts et Métiers** *(p.43)*, botanists and zoologists based at the **Jardin des Plantes** *(p.114)*, while digital technology has the edge at the **Gaîté Lyrique** *(p.42)*.

## ... Parisian chic

If there's one word that is instantly associated with *Parisiennes*, it is 'chic'. An inimitable *je ne sais quoi* is achieved with the perfect accoutrements – perhaps a sublime handbag from **Balenciaga** *(p.70)* or exclusive scent from **Les Salons du Palais Royal-Shiseido** *(p.52)*, the indulgence of a chocolate wrap in the Spa at the **Four Seasons George V** *(p.79)*, elegantly packaged gâteaux from the **Pâtisserie des Rêves** *(p.142)*, lunch at **Mini Palais** *(p.69)*, discovering the secret **Salon du Panthéon** *(p.122)*, or joining ladies who tea at the **Musée Jacquemart-André** *(p.72)*.

# neighbourhoods

With the River Seine running through the middle, Paris divides neatly into Right Bank *(Rive Droite)* to the north, traditionally associated with business and commerce, and intellectual, literary Left Bank *(Rive Gauche)* to the south; a collection of villages each with its own style, though a more truthful divide would perhaps be between wealthy west and poorer, working-class east.

**The Islands and the Marais** In the heart of the city yet a world apart: Ile de la Cité is the centre of religious and legal Paris, while Ile St-Louis is a genteel 17th-century enclave. Across the water on the Right Bank, the Marais district was built up in the 16th and 17th centuries and happily escaped most of Baron Haussmann's urban projects – leaving intact stunning mansions of golden stone now colonised by gay bars, fashion boutiques and art galleries.

**Louvre, Opéra and Grands Boulevards** The Louvre and Palais Garnier opera house epitomise the Paris of great royal and imperial monuments. But you'll also find entertainment along the Grands Boulevards, unusual covered passages traversing the financial district behind Palais Royal, and historic rue St-Honoré, a great shopping street.

**Champs-Elysées and Monceau** The Champs-Elysées is flashy Paris, all luxury shops, lavish apartments and grand hotels. The area was transformed by the world fairs, and the flamboyant Grand Palais and the museums of Chaillot hill which came in their wake. Monceau is a monied, less showy area, concealing a romantic park and chic museums.

**Montmartre and Pigalle** Montmartre does its best to convince you it's a rural hill village. More urban Pigalle, long associated with sleaze, is still a nightlife focus. To the south, little explored Nouvelle Athènes, two centuries ago an intellectual hub, and the gritty Gare du Nord hinterland are experiencing a bar and bobo *(bourgeois bohémien)* revival.

**Bastille, Belleville and Ménilmontant** Bastille is the historic furniture-making district, peppered with craft workshops and symbol of the Revolution. Multicultural Ménilmontant and Belleville seem far from the Paris of Haussmann, with wildly contrasting public housing and villagey pockets. Here you'll find Père Lachaise cemetery, a new gallery district and cultural venues with an underground edge.

**Latin Quarter, St-Germain and Seine** The Latin Quarter is historically the university quarter, where you'll find Roman remains, medieval streets, studenty bars and art cinemas mixed in with prestigious academic institutions and some of the city's loveliest churches. St-Germain is quintessential, international Left Bank, synonymous with café society, although a chic fashion set has rather replaced its literary clients.

**Invalides and Montparnasse** To the east of Les Invalides, the mansions of Faubourg-St-Germain are home to ministries and discreet *vieux France* aristocracy; to the west is bourgeois residential territory, which often means good places to eat, plus a few oddities like the Eiffel Tower. Montparnasse spelled cosmopolitan, artistic Paris in the 1920s, and while the Montparnasse Tower changed the skyline, the district is still popular for its brasseries and cinemas.

**Beyond the Centre** Heterogenous, outlying Paris includes villagey Charonne, smart Auteuil and urban renewal in Chinatown and at La Villette. Parisians tend to be disdainful of the suburbs, but nearby St-Denis, Vincennes and St-Cloud all have royal connections; attractions range from a castle to a football stadium; and there are signs that Paris is beginning to look beyond its frontiers and envisage the creation of a Grand Paris.

# The Islands and the Marais

# Eyeball the **medieval gargoyles** at **Notre-Dame**

Climbing the spiral staircase up the north tower of *Notre-Dame* and emerging onto the gallery high up on the west front, eye to eye with the gargoyles and chimeras, there is probably no better place to reflect on the skill of the medieval stonemason and the faith that made this one of France's great Gothic cathedrals. An additional hike takes you up the south tower past the giant bourdon bell and onto the roof itself, to be met by the view immortalised in the brilliant 1939 film version of Victor Hugo's *The Hunchback of Notre-Dame* – where Charles Laughton scuttles across the rooftop as Quasimodo. In fact, the original French title of the book is *Notre-Dame de Paris*, which suggests that the true hero of the tale is the cathedral itself. Hugo was passionate about the monument he called 'the queen of cathedrals', though he complained about its decrepit, mutilated state – the result of centuries of weathering, 'improvements' and Revolutionary destruction – and campaigned for its restoration.

Restoration was finally launched in the 1840s by fervent Gothic Revivalist Eugène Viollet-le-Duc. Some of his chimeras are no doubt too Gothic to be true but the works did save the cathedral, famed – despite a rather gloomy interior – for its three richly carved portals, its rose windows and massive flying buttresses.

This is Paris's most visited monument, and yet still very much a place of worship: used for services and organ recitals, state funerals and a vast procession for August's Fête de l'Assomption.

*Cathédrale Notre-Dame de Paris; parvis de Notre-Dame; tel: 01 42 34 56 10; towers tel: 01 53 10 07 00; www.notre damedeparis.fr; Mon–Fri 8am-6.45pm, Sat–Sun 8am-7.15pm, towers Apr–Sept daily 10am-6.30pm, May–Aug until 11pm Sat–Sun, Oct–Mar daily 10am-5.30pm; free, charge for towers; map B3*

# Read **stained-glass stories** at the **Sainte-Chapelle**

When Louis IX purchased the Crown of Thorns and some fragments of the True Cross from the impoverished Emperor Baldwin II in Constantinople, for 135,000 livres in 1239, he instantly boosted his prestige and saintly reputation as well as that of Paris. The king then set about building a suitably magnificent receptacle for his precious relics, erecting the double-decker Sainte Chapelle in record speed between 1242 and 1248 in the heart of the royal palace.

A gem of Flamboyant Gothic architecture, the chapel is all the more jewel-like for being hidden from the street within the Palais de Justice, Paris's central law courts, so that you often encounter two queues snaking along – one for the chapel and one for those waiting to sit in on trials.

Between the chapel's two levels, a striking contrast operates. The lower chapel, originally for the use of palace servants, is dark and intimate, with an early fresco of the Annunciation and its vaulted ceiling painted with fleur de lys against the blue of a night sky. Conversely, arrive in the upper chapel, once reserved for the royal family and clergy, and you are thrown into the light glinting off pale stone and the dappled reflections, all deep blues and ruby reds, from the stained glass windows that seem to take up almost all of the chapel's upper section. In a jigsaw of small intensely coloured pieces, most of its original, minuscule figures depict 1,113 scenes from the Old Testament and the Crucifixion, to be read from the bottom up, while one window recounts the story of the relics themselves.

*Sainte Chapelle; 4 boulevard du Palais; tel: 01 53 40 60 80; http://sainte-chapelle.monuments-nationaux.fr; Mar–June, Sept–Oct daily 9.30am–1pm, 2.15–6pm, July–Aug daily 9.30am–6pm, Nov–Feb daily 9am–1pm, 2.15–5pm; charge, bring ID; map A4*

# Feal the fear in the cells of the condemned at the **Conciergerie**, Marie-Antoinette's last dwelling place

Many people bypass the Conciergerie for the Sainte Chapelle – which is a pity, for the surprisingly extensive remains of the Capetian kings' medieval palace are a rare example of secular Gothic architecture and also one of the sights that best evokes the French Revolution.

Entry is directly into the Salle des Gens d'Armes, an impressive vaulted hall nearly 70 metres (70 yards) long where a slab of black marble mounted on the wall is a remnant of one of the long tables used for banquets in the Great Hall above.

When the royals took up residence at Vincennes and the Louvre, the palace became a prison under the control of the Concierge; the second part of the visit reflects this gory episode. During the Revolution, hundreds passed by here on their way to the guillotine, condemned by the Tribunal Révolutionnaire whose members included the revolutionary Robespierre – who himself fell victim to the Terror in 1794.

A handful of the cells have been re-created to show how conditions varied according to status or income: from the *paillasse*, the communal area where poorer prisoners slept on *paille* (straw) on the floor, via the *pistole* for those who could pay for beds, to the cells of the privileged or wealthy, kitted out with desks and lamps even. The probable location of the cell where Marie-Antoinette spent two months before execution now holds a chapel.

Exhibits include busts of Robespierre, keys, locks and a guillotine blade which hangs from the wall – understated but chilling.

*Conciergerie; 2 boulevard du Palais; tel: 01 53 40 60 80; http://conciergerie. monuments-nationaux.fr, daily 9.30am–5.30pm; charge; map B4*

# Pay tribute to the past in the **two crypts on Ile de la Cité**

For an idea of what the Ile de la Cité was like before Baron Haussmann knocked down the clutter of medieval houses in front of Notre Dame, descend into the **Crypte Archéologique** located under the parvis of the cathedral, an in-situ archaeological dig that takes you back centuries through the island's Roman and medieval past. There's a stretch of Roman quayside and bits of ramparts, the hypocaust from a bathing complex, medieval shop cellars, stairways, pavements, traces of a foundling hospital and a 19th-century sewer, all in a complicated layering which piled up as the ground level rose with all the debris.

At the other end of the cathedral, steps lead down to a very different sort of crypt: the **Mémorial des Martyrs de la Déportation**, a dignified monument to World War II deportees. Inaugurated in 1962, Georges-Henri Pingusson's architecture of iron bars and geometrical blocks of roughened white concrete is an ecumenical crypt in memory of all the Jews, Communists, homosexuals, gypsies and Resistance fighters who were deported from France. In the shrine you'll find fragments of glass recalling the thousands of deportees, side galleries with triangular niches containing earth and cinders from the concentration camps, quotations from poems by Eluard, Aragon, Desnos, Sartre and Saint-Exupéry, and the inscription, 'forgive but don't forget'.

*Crypte Archéologique; 7 parvis Notre-Dame; tel: 01 55 42 50 10; http://crypte. paris.fr; Tue–Sun 10am–6pm, last admission 5.30pm, charge; map B3 Mémorial des Martyrs de la Déportation; square de l'Ile de France; tel: 01 46 33 87 56; Apr–Sept daily 10am–noon, 2–7pm, Oct–Mar daily 10am–noon, 2–5pm; free; map C3*

# Stroll along a **17th-century high street** on secluded **Ile St-Louis**

The picture of insular insouciance in the middle of the Seine, Ile St-Louis is a 17th-century timewarp that appears to have barely changed since it was created as a property venture between developer Christophe Marie and royal architect Louis Le Vau. Today, the island remains a highly desirable residential address and a lovely place for a stroll, its *quais* lined with elegant houses and bisected as it is by exclusive high street rue St-Louis-en-l'Ile. As on any self-respecting high street, here you'll find food shops (rather superior ones, of course) including a foie gras specialist, places to eat and tempting gift shops, most of which are open on Sunday. Notable for their curiosity factor are the Hôtel du Jeu de Paume at No. 54, where rooms lead off a wood-framed *jeu de paume* (a real tennis court); and the leering dragons holding up the balcony of the Hôtel Chenizot, at No. 51 (during the week you can walk into the courtyard where there's another fine facade with sunburst motif).

The eastern section of the street is home to **Berthillon** (No. 31; tel: 01 43 54 31 61), Paris's most famous *glacier*. On the western side, temptations include Provençal soaps and perfumes at **Durance** (No. 37) , chocolates at **Cacao et Chocolat** (No. 63), chunky resin jewellery at **Sobral** (No. 79), gifts and gadgets at **Pylones** (No. 57) and old-fashioned toys at **L'Arche de Noé** (No. 70). Stylish bistro **Mon Vieil Ami** (No. 69; tel: 01 40 46 01 35) is the most sophisticated place to eat, while flanking the Pont St-Louis – the footbridge leading to the Ile de la Cité – are Alsatian stalwart **La Brasserie de l'Isle St-Louis** (*pictured*; tel: 01 43 54 02 59), and tea room cum café **Le Flore en l'Ile** (tel: 01 43 29 88 27), renowned for its rich hot chocolate far too thick to pour.

*Ile St-Louis; map C3–D4*

# Discover sculptures and colonnades in the grand
## courtyards of the Marais

The Marais *hôtel particulier* (grand private townhouse) was the des res of 17th-century nobles and civil servants who needed to be in town near the royal court, typically in a fine house set behind an entrance courtyard, with wings, the requisite stabling and formal gardens at the rear. When the Marais fell from fashion the houses became industrial premises and tenements, but many have now been beautifully restored. Several are museums, including **Hôtel Carnavalet** *(p.33)*, **Hôtel Guénégaud** *(p.35)*, **Hôtel de St-Aignan** *(p.36)*, **Hôtel Donon** (Musée Cognacq Jay, 8 rue Elzévir; map D4), and **Hôtel Salé;** (map D5), now the Picasso museum (5 rue Thorigny; www.musee-picasso.fr; closed until 2013). Others house galleries, shops, schools, even the fire station on rue de Sévigné. Everywhere, you can spot fine doorways and carved heads, and during the week, you can often wander into its courtyards.

Cross through the **Hôtel de Sully** between 62 rue St-Antoine and the place des Vosges; (map D/E3) to admire sculpted facades representing the elements and the seasons. **Hôtel Lamoignan** (24 rue Pavée; map D4), now the Paris history library but

built in the 1580s for Diane de France, daughter of Henri II, has a Renaissance courtyard with giant order pilasters and Greek key motifs. On rue des Francs-Bourgeois, lined with numerous 17th- and 18th-century mansions, the **Hôtel de Soubise** *(pictured;* No. 60; tel: 01 40 27 60 96; map C5), now the National Archives, has a glorious colonnaded *cour d'honneur* (main courtyard). The real treat here, however, are its grand rococo interiors decorated in the 1730s by Van Loo, Lemoyne, Restout and Natoire for the Prince de Soubise; the Salon du Prince is used for concerts on Saturdays, while its newly restored gardens connect to the **Hôtel de Rohan** (map D5), built for one of the prince's sons and famed for its relief *The Stallions of the Sun*.

# Drop in on **Victor Hugo** at his very personal apartment on **place des Vosges**

Henri IV had plenty of town planning schemes for Paris, and in 1605, with the glorious arcaded **place des Vosges** (originally place Royale), he got it just right: a symmetrical square with 34 identical pavilions punctuated by the Pavillon de la Reine on one side and the Pavillon du Roi on the other. Its Flemish Renaissance-influenced style has been attributed to the Métezeau brothers, who designed the remarkably similar place Ducale in Charleville-Mezières. In fact the pavilions in red brick with stone chaining and steep slate roofs are just a facade – look closely and you'll see that on some the brick is imitation – and plots of various sizes were sold off behind to assorted royal officials and entrepreneurs. As for the gardens in the centre, they were created in the 1630s complete with an equestrian statue of Louis XIII, though the railings, trees, fountains and playgrounds came later on.

Victor Hugo had the good fortune to live on the square when he, along with his wife and four children, rented an apartment on the second floor of the Hôtel de Rohan-Guéménée, now the **Maison de Victor Hugo**, from 1832 to 1848. Here he would write many of his poems and several novels, including *Marie Tudor* and *Ruy Blas*. A series of rooms evokes different periods of his life and his numerous passions, including the eccentric pseudo-medieval dining room furniture he designed for long-standing mistress Juliette Drouet when in exile in Guernsey (after opposing Napoleon III's coup d'état), and his enthusiasm for the newfangled art of photography.

*Maison de Victor Hugo; 6 place des Vosges; tel: 01 42 72 10 16; www.paris.fr; Tue–Sun 10am–6pm; free; map E3*

# Sift through time at Paris's eclectic historical museum, **Musée Carnavalet**

Paris's history museum is slightly chaotic and could do with some reorganisation. Having said that, as you sift through the sheer number of exhibits and a confusing route not helped by a complicated layout over two linked mansions, the museum's eclecticism is also its fascination: curiously, this clutter somehow conveys an impression of the plurality of Parisian history and its population of shopkeepers and artisans, clergy and nobles, revolutionaries and royalists, mondaines and writers.

Start by admiring the courtyard facade of Hôtel Carnavalet, Paris's finest Renaissance house built

in 1584, with relief figures of the four seasons attributed to sculptor Jean Goujon, who also worked on the Louvre. The entrance to the museum brings you straight into a gallery full of vivid wrought iron shop signs, but it's worth taking a detour to the Orangerie, which houses Neolithic dugout canoes discovered at Bercy.

Some of the most interesting items are souvenirs of the French Revolution, ranging from a gaming table made from a block of the Bastille fortress to lockets containing Louis XVI and Marie-Antoinette's hair. There are also souvenirs of Madame de Sévigné, famed for her gossipy letters describing court life, who lived here from 1677-96.

After the Revolution, the *belle époque* is much more festive: Marcel Proust's bedroom, two fabulous Art Nouveau rooms, the ballroom of Wenzel with paintings entirely covering walls and ceiling, and Alphonse Mucha's peacock-filled shop for jeweller Georges Fouquet.

*Musée Carnavalet; 23 rue de Sévigné; tel: 01 44 59 58 58; http://carnavalet. paris.fr; Tue–Sun 10am–6pm; collection free, charge for exhibitions; map D4*

# Ride the iconic escalators at powerhouse for modern art and architecture the **Centre Pompidou**

A fabulous intrusion in the Parisian cityscape, the **Centre Pompidou** – named after French president Georges Pompidou (1911–74) – catapaulted architects Richard Rogers and Renzo Piano to fame; more than 30 years after opening, it's still one of the most exciting buildings in Paris and a savvy extension of the urban environment. Going for the boiler house look meant that all service conduits and escalators were located on the outside, leaving the inside free for moveable walls. Crucially, this was also a boiler house of interaction, setting a pluridisciplinary model that has since been aped the world over. The airy central forum leads to an art museum, exhibition galleries, auditoria, cinema, reference library and experimental music institute. There are special galleries for

children and teenagers and a full cultural programme on offer.

The permanent collection of the **Musée National d'Art Moderne** gives an unrivalled picture of the history of modern art from 1906 to the present, from Fauvism to multimedia. Only a fragment of the collection is shown at a time; but upstairs in the historical section, you can be sure to find Picasso, Braque and the Cubists, superb works by Matisse, the birth of abstraction with Kandinsky and the Delaunays, Malevich, one-off individuals like Rouault or Francis Bacon, Dada including Duchamp's iconic *Fountain*, Surrealist paintings, and the wall from André Breton's apartment with his collection of tribal art.

On the floor below it's Pop and nouveau réalisme, arte povera and conceptual art, video art and installations, Warhol's *Ten Lizzes* or a giant mushroom by Carsten Holler. Big prestigious exhibitions are held on the sixth floor, next to the slinky aluminium pods of restaurant Georges, great anytime or a buzzy nightime destination for people-watching with a view.

*Centre Pompidou; tel: 01 44 78 33 12; www.centrepompidou.fr; Wed–Mon 11am–9pm; charge; map C5*

# Track down a bestiary at the **Musée de la Chasse et de la Nature**

On the same premises as an aristocratic hunting club, this eccentric museum dedicated to nature and the hunt has been imaginatively renovated in the beautiful Hôtel de Guénégaud (designed by François Mansart in 1651-55 for the king's secretary, Jean-François Guénéguad des Brosses) and the adjacent Hôtel de Mongelas (1705). This is an intriguing museum if only because gauging where it stands – somewhere between animal lover and fervent hunter, as seen out in the autumnal French countryside – can be quite tricky. But that's part of the point: this is an exploration of the image of the wild animal, man's relation to nature, and the inspiration animals have given to the fine and decorative arts.

Much of the museum is arranged roughly by species, with rooms dedicated to wild boar, deer, dogs, wolves and even a cabinet of curiosities on the mythical unicorn. Slightly scary stuffed tigers and a massive rampant bear inhabit one room, another is full of beautifully crafted shotguns, bows and spears. There are old masters by Cranach and Snyders, painted porcelain tea services and animal-shaped porcelain tureens, and a large collection of Desportes' vivid oil sketches of animals, as well as his portrait of Diane and Blond, Louis XIV's favourite hunting dogs.

The museum has also integrated works by contemporary artists, such as photos by Eric Poitevin, a Jeff Koons' porcelain *Puppy* and, in a tiny panelled room containing two panels by Rubens and Velvet Brueghel, a mysterious owl feather ceiling by Belgian artist Jan Fabre – where beady eyes stare down at you from above.

*Musée de la Chasse et de la Nature; 62 rue des Archives; tel: 01 53 01 92 40; www.chassenature.org; Tue–Sun 11am–6pm; charge; map D5*

# Choose between **cheesecake and falafel** in the **Jewish Marais**

If the Marais' Jewish community, the *pletzl*, originally largely consisted of Ashkenazy Jews – first from Alsace after the emancipation brought by the Revolution, later fleeing the pogroms in Eastern Europe at the end of the 19th century – more recently it has been joined by Sephardic Jews from North Africa following the end of French colonisation. This cosmopolitan mix of origins is satisfyingly summed up in rue des Rosiers, where the traditional bakers, delis and Judaica shops of central Europe mingle with North African falafel joints, amid the ever-encroaching fashion boutiques. Try **Sacha Finkelstajn** (*pictured*; No. 27; tel: 01 42 72 78 91) for plaited hallah bread, poppyseed cake, excellent cheesecake, strudel, perojskis, dill peppers and hot salt beef sandwiches; and the **As du Fallafel** (No. 34; tel: 01 48 87 63 60) for spicy tahina-laden falafel to take away or eat at a handful of tables. Around the corner, the synogogue at 10 rue Pavée was designed in 1913 by Hector Guimard, better known for his Art Nouveau metro entrances.

At the **Musée d'Art et d'Histoire du Judaïsme**, Jewish history is treated not only as a history of diasporas and religious ceremonies, but as a history of art and the decorative arts too. Displayed in the beautifully restored 17th-century Hôtel de Saint-Aignan, the collection includes torah scrolls and hannukah lamps, a wooden synagogue from Austria, artefacts from the printing tradition along with fabulous Baroque silverware from Holland, and ornate costumes and jewellery from North Africa and Turkey. After dealing with Jewish communities and traditions around the world, the gallery turns its focus onto Jews in France after the Revolution, the Dreyfus case, intellectual life and an impressive array of paintings and sculptures by Jewish artists of the Ecole de Paris – such as Chagall, Modigliani, Lipchitz and Chana Orloff. The museum deliberately does not cover the Holocaust, although a work by artist Christian Boltanski in a narrow courtyard recalls the numerous Jewish families who were living in flats in this very building in 1939.

Instead, the Holocaust is remembered at the **Mémorial de la Shoah**. Enter past the Wall of Names, the list of 76,000 Jews deported from France of whom only about 2,500 survived, despite the best efforts of the *justes* who hid and helped Jews in France during the war – more than 2,000 *justes* are listed on an external wall along the Allée des Justes. Inside is a crypt containing the Memorial to the Unknown Jewish Martyr, with an eternal flame burning at the centre of a marble star of David and a room of chillingly meticulous police files kept by the Vichy regime. The memorial was extended in 2005 with a sober but not melodramatic presentation of the history of the deportations and concentration camps in France and the rest of Europe. Photographs, letters, newspaper clippings and film interviews of survivors highlight personal stories against the broad current of events, ending with a moving wall of photos of France's 3,000 child deportees.

*Musée d'Art et d'Histoire du Judaïsme; 71 rue du Temple; tel: 01 53 01 86 60; www.mahj.org; Mon-Fri 11am-6pm, Sun 10am-6pm; charge; map C5 Mémorial de la Shoah; 17 rue Geoffrey l'Asnier; tel: 01 42 77 44 72; www.memorialdelashoah.org; Sun-Fri 10am-6pm, Thur until 10pm; free; map C3*

# Browse in the **junk shops of Village St-Paul**, a labyrinth of tucked-away courtyards

Between the rue St-Antoine and the river sits St-Paul, a less frenzied district away from the hype and continual fashion parade of the northern Marais. **Eglise St-Paul** (99 rue St-Antoine) is a Counter-Reformation church modelled on the Gesù in Rome with an impressive skylit dome; exit from a side door and an alley leads to rue St-Paul. Follow the road down to a series of archways through which lies the labyrinth of interconnected courtyards of the **Village St-Paul**, home to antiques dealers and *brocantes*, where eclectic wares run from vintage furniture to wine gadgets. A handful of cafés and bistros include **Cru**, for raw food

buffs, whilst on rue des Jardins-St-Paul, the longest visible section of Philippe Augustus's city wall, built 1190 and with a watchtower, runs down the side of a sports ground.

Back on rue St-Paul is the discreet entrance of the **Musée de la Magie**, prized by children and prestidigitators. Distorting mirrors, optical illusions and a couple of trunks for cutting ladies in half are displayed around vaulted cellars. Visits include a magic show.

While in the area take a look at the melodramatically turreted **Hôtel de Sens** (1 rue Figuier; www.paris.fr); along with the Hôtel de Cluny, this rare surviving Gothic mansion is a precursor of the Marais *hôtel particulier* (p.31). Nearby, the **Maison Européenne de la Photographie** is a great photography space and its minimalist modern extension, with frequently changing shows of historic and contemporary photography, features an unusual collection of Polaroids.

*Musée de la Magie; 11 rue St-Paul; tel: 01 42 72 13 26; www.museedelamagie.com; Wed, Sat, Sun 2–7pm; charge; map D3*
*Maison Européenne de la Photographie, 5 rue de Fourcy; tel: 01 44 78 75 00; www.mep-fr.org; Wed–Sun 11am–8pm; charge; map D4*

# **Gallery hop** on rue de Turenne and rue Vieille-du-Temple

If there's one thing you can be sure of, it's that the art world will turn out for a *vernissage* (private view) at the dynamic **Galerie Perrotin** (76 rue de Turenne; tel: 01 42 16 79 79; www.perrotin.com; map E5), one of the city's most happening art galleries. Here you can expect big showy pieces from a trendy international list studded with the likes of Takashi Murakami, Maurizio Cattelan and Bharti Kher, and French artists Sophie Calle, Xavier Veilhan and Kolkoz. Emmanuel Perrotin began showing artists in his flat twenty years ago. He now occupies three floors of a Marais mansion, an adjacent industrial brick building and another gallery across the street behind. Around the corner, powerhouse **Galerie Yvon Lambert** (108 rue Vieille-du-Temple; tel: 01 42 71 09 33; www.yvon-lambert.com; map D5) was one of the first to move to the Marais from the traditional gallery base in St-Germain and still shows famous names such as Jenny Holzer, Nan Goldin or Anselm Kiefer, along with younger stars Douglas Gordon, Jonathan Monk and Loris Gréaud. Another must on the art circuit is **Chantal Crousel** (*pictured*; 10 rue Charlot; tel: 01 42 77 38 87; www.crousel.com; map D5) for interesting installation and video art from artists including Mona Hatoum, Thomas Hirschhorn, Anri Sala or Rirkrit Tiravanija – who constructed an entire wooden barge here. At **Chez Valentin** (9 rue St-Gilles; tel: 01 48 87 42 55; www.galeriechezvalentin.com; map E4) shows tend to be complex and conceptual; while **Almine Rech** (19 rue Saintonge; tel: 01 45 83 71 90; www.alminerech.com; map D5) shows painters and photographers, often with minimalist tendencies, around the whitewashed rooms of an old house.

To see what shows are on or coming up, pick up the *Galeries mode d'emploi* leaflet in one of the galleries or check out www.fondation-entreprise-ricard.com and www.paris-art.com.

# Hang out with the fashionistas in the Haut-Marais

With its one-off boutiques and quirky mix of hip labels, vintage discoveries and rising designers, the Haut-Marais (map D4-5, E5-6) has become an essential destination for the fashion pack. Entered through a period doorway, **L'Eclaireur** (40 rue de Sévigné; tel: 01 48 87 10 22; www.leclaireur.com) is worth a look as much for the extraordinary interior of cascading planks and flickering video screens by Belgian artist-architect Arne Quinze as for its hip selection of luxury womenswear and bags by Céline, Balenciaga or Gareth Pugh. However, the real hub for those on the fashion trail is to be found around the junction of rue Vieille-du-Temple and rue de Poitou. Here, the mix of contemporary art galleries and independent fashion shops is typified at 108 rue Vieille-du-Temple, where Galerie Yvon Lambert *(p.39)* cohabits with adventurous clothes and accessories from design, fashion and advertising collective **Surface to Air** (tel: 01 44 61 76 27; www.surfacetoair.com). Check out the women's fashion selection at **Abou d'Abi Bazar** (125 rue Vieille-du-Temple; tel: 01 42 71 13 26; www.aboudabibazar.com) and the

trendy upmarket labels, such as Marc by Marc Jacobs and See by Chloé, at its neighbour **Shine** (15 rue de Poitou; tel: 01 48 05 80 10), on the corner with rue de Poitou. As well as the **Hôtel du Petit Moulin** *(p.172)* – the first hotel designed by fashion maestro Christian Lacroix – Rue de Poitou has a throng of interesting outlets, such as **Swildens** (No. 22; tel: 01 42 71 19 12; www.swildens.fr), for casual yet chic streamlined clothes and rock chick bags by up and coming designer Juliette Swildens. Meanwhile **Matières à Réflexion** at No. 19 (tel: 01 42 72 16 31; www.matieresareflexion.com) brings together the trends for vintage and recycling, where old leather jackets are turned into characterful handbags – you can even take in your own beloved leather jacket for a customised version. The window displays are always particularly good at **Christophe Lemaire** (No. 28; tel: 01 44 78 00 09; www.christophelemaire.com), a boutique set in an old corner pharmacy, where Lemaire, the new womenswear designer for Hermès, shows off his own flowing Japanese-influenced men's and women's lines. Don't miss **Isabel Marant** (47 rue de

Saintonge; tel: 01 42 78 19 24; www.isabelmarant.tm.fr) either for her quirky yet wearable threads with a neo-hippie look and ethnic touches.

Fashionistas take a breather and refreshments at trendy corner café **Le Progrès** (1 rue de Bretagne; tel: 01 42 72 01 44) and at **Café Charlot** (38 rue de Bretagne; tel: 01 44 54 03 30), a new hotspot in a converted bakery, or tuck into sweet and savoury pancakes in the beach shack setting of Paris's most fashionable crêperie,

**Breizh Café** (109 rue Vieille-du-Temple; tel: 01 42 72 13 77; www.breizhcafe.com). Tying all the strands together is **Merci** (111 boulevard Beaumarchais; tel: 01 42 77 00 33; www.merci-merci.com): three storeys of artfully distressed industrial space where you'll find a brilliantly eclectic choice of new and pre-owned clothes, furniture, kitchen items, hardware, perfumes and light switches. You can stop for lunch downstairs or sip a coffee in Merci's café cum secondhand bookstore.

# Lose yourself in **electronic soundscapes** at digitally daring the **Gaîté Lyrique**

An ornate 19th-century facade of red marble and grandiose columns hides the **Gaîté Lyrique**, recently reborn as a daring new cultural centre with a mission to bring you all that is up to the minute in electronic arts and digital technology. The building itself has had a chequered history, from its glorious origins as the theatre where some of Offenbach's operettas were first performed to an ill-fated attempt to turn it into a theme park in the 1980s, when most of the old interior was ripped out. Only the grand foyer, now hung with flying-saucer lights and concealed speakers, remains from 1862, leaving a concrete shell for seven storeys of auditoria, galleries, cafés, a boutique, and rehearsal and recording studios. You'll notice colourful modules that can be perambulated around the building and serve as everything from individual video-screening booths to offices and cloakrooms; as well as white polyhedric blocks that can be assembled into seats, bars and information counters, or illuminated as lamps. The Gaîté Lyrique has an admirably broad vision of digital culture, a desire to make it accessible to everyone and an international approach. Since its opening in spring 2011, it has invited artists and photographers, musicians and skateboarders – this one-time theatre is turning out to be a surprisingly apt setting for a decidedly theatrical approach. The Gaîté's programme includes not only concerts but debates and brunches, performance and DJs, a padded booth for listening to electronic soundworks, a computer gaming room, and art installations that react as you walk past them.

*Gaîté Lyrique; 3 bis rue Papin; tel: 01 53 01 51 51; www.gaite-lyrique.net; Tue–Sat 2–8pm, Sun 2–6pm, concert times vary; map C7*

# Tune into technology at **Musée des Arts et Métiers**

Unlike the pure-science emphasis adopted by Paris's other science museums, the unusual **Musée des Arts et Métiers** is more about engineering and inventions, set amid the striking architecture of the medieval priory of Saint-Martin-des-Champs. The museum was founded in 1794 by the Abbé Grégoire, a member of the Revolutionary Convention, to train engineers and technicians; the rails by which pieces of apparatus were trundled off to lecture halls for demonstration are still visible in the parquet flooring. There are sections devoted to mechanics and materials, construction and communications, from astrolabes and Pascal's calculator to TVs, computers and a 60's jukebox, not to mention a collection of elaborate 18th-century musical automatons. Most spectacular of the displays is undoubtedly the cars and aeroplanes in the nave, including the plane in which Louis Blériot made the first flight across the Channel in 1909. Some of the most memorable items, however, are those inventions that didn't quite work, such as Clément Ader's fragile bat-like plane that hangs in the grand stairway, flying rather more successfully now than when it hopped along the ground in 1890. Keeping up the steam theme is a good café, A Toutes Vapeurs, specialising in steamed dishes.

*Musée des Arts et Métiers; 60 rue Réaumur; tel: 01 53 01 82 00; www.arts-et-metiers.net; Tue–Sun 10am–6pm, Thur until 9.30pm; charge; map C7*

# Louvre, Opéra & Grands Boulevards

# Louvre, Opéra and Grands Boulevards

# Pick a side in the battle of **Romantics versus Classicists** at **the Louvre**

Pitting the two rival tendancies in late 18th and early 19th century painting – neoclassicists and romantics, line versus colour – the Grande Galerie sums up French art in all its grandeur. A period when French artists were impassioned observers or even participants in current events (with an eye for dressing things up in mythology), it's a perfect preview before tackling the rest of the museum. On one side, you'll find the political neoclassicism of David's *Oath of the Horatii* and *Sacre de Napoléon*, where the emperor is crowned in Notre Dame before a cast of millions. While across the hallway comes the flamboyance, emotion, motion and colour of Romanticism: Delacroix's *Liberty Leading the People*, where the tricolore-bearing figure of Marianne is as much a bravura manifesto as a depiction of the Revolution, and his delightfully daft and bloodthirsty *Death of Sardanopolus*.

As the world's largest museum, you could spend months here, and even though the throng often almost blocks the view of the *Mona Lisa*, take a small staircase and you can suddenly find yourself alone. So, allow yourself to get a little lost to make your own discoveries: unlikely attics with battle scenes by Charles Le Brun, Rubens' vast cycle of the *Life of Marie de Médicis* that contrasts with two sparkling, loving portraits of his wife, or small rooms containing gems of northern painting such as Vermeer's *The Lacemaker*. For all its size, the Louvre is surprisingly user-friendly, though be sure to pick up a map in the entrance hall.

*Musée du Louvre; rue de Rivoli; tel: 01 40 20 50 50; www.louvre.fr, Wed–Mon 10am–6pm, Wed and Fri until 9.45pm; charge; map E2*

# **Shop** where revolutionaries once plotted in the arcades around **Palais-Royal**

For evidence of how even the most historic-looking districts are continually being reinvented, you only have to visit the arcades surrounding the Palais-Royal gardens. What had been a sleepy backwater selling musical boxes and medals has shot into the superleague of adventurous fashion. Almost side by side on Galerie de Valois are **Pierre Hardy** (No. 156), for streetwise yet intellectual men's and women's shoes (think Mondrian on feet); the arty/distressed look of **Rick Owens** (No. 133); and the huge **Stella McCartney** store (No. 121). Galerie Montpensier has the **Marc Jacobs** empire (No. 34) and **Didier Ludot** (No. 24), guru of vintage fashion.

Just the rustle of shopping bags disturbs the calm of the gardens, a lovely oasis in the heart of Paris. While the palace itself (now the Conseil d'Etat and Ministry of Culture) was built in the 1630s for Cardinal Richelieu, the galleries were added in the 18th-century, becoming a place where high life met low life in gambling dens and cafés. At Café Foy, Camille Desmoulins called upon his comrades to storm the Bastille prison on 13 July 1789, marking the start of the Revolution. The Café de Chartres, opened in 1784, is now

the splendid **Grand Véfour** (17 rue de Beaujolais; tel: 01 42 96 56 27; www.grand-vefour.com) with fine cuisine, period interiors and its old name still visible on the facade.

Admire Daniel Buren's **black and white columns** in the palace courtyard. The artwork caused a stir when installed in 1986 but has become a favourite spot for sitting on, hopping on or dropping a coin.

Another curiosity is the midday cannon. Made by a clockmaker in 1786, it fired every day at noon, triggered by the sun passing the Paris meridien, allowing Parisians to set their watches. The original was stolen in 1998, but a replica goes off every Wednesday.

*Palais-Royal; map E2–3*

# Eat a **truly Parisian lunch**, from regionally sourced ingredients, at gastro temple **Le Meurice**

One of the usual glories of Parisian cuisine is its wealth of ingredients drawn from all over France, from mountain to Mediterranean; but for lunch at **Le Meurice**, it's all about going back to local roots. Here amid the gilding, blowsy neo-rococo ceiling and crystal chandeliers of the very grand dining room, three-star Michelin chef Yannick Alléno has created the wonderful Déjeuner du Terroir Parisien (lunch based on ingredients sourced from the Paris region) alongside the more expected lobster, turbot and caviar *à la carte*. Alléno is proud of his Parisian origins, privileging produce from local producers who devotedly cultivate old varieties, and rediscovering long-forgotten regional recipes – whilst endowing them with a gastro flourish. It's rural Ile de France meets grand gastronomy: 'I find my inspiration in the capital, its history, its mythic places, and through the encounters they provoke. I work with Parisian terroir because a typically Parisian cuisine is at the origin of French gastronomy.'

A typical lunch menu might include Montmorency cherries, saffron from the Gâtinais, asparagus cultivated and hand picked in Pontoise, and sole with a *duxelles* of *champignons de Paris* – button mushrooms still raised in dark, dank former stone quarries.

*Le Meurice; 228 rue de Rivoli; tel: 01 44 58 10 55; www.lemeurice.com; L and D Mon–Fri, closed Aug; map C3*

---

**OTHER FLAVOURS FROM THE ILE-DE-FRANCE REGION**
Other regional specialities include brie and creamy fontainebleau cheeses, particularly good from **Barthélémy** (51 rue de Grenelle; tel: 01 42 22 82 24), while at the **Fromagerie Mouffetard** (131 rue Mouffetard; tel 01 47 07 18 15), you can find brie not just from Meaux and Melun but also Montereau and Provins. Meanwhile, honey production is a growing phenomenon, with hives installed on the roofs of the Palais Garnier and Grand Palais among other places.

# Gaze down through decades of interior design at the
## Musée des Arts Décoratifs

The top of the turret makes a good start to exploring the **Musée des Arts Décoratifs**: an astonishing view along rue de Rivoli out through bull's eye windows coupled with, internally, a visual descent through the decades of 20th-century design – from the 1940s on the 9th floor, via a pyramid of 1960s' chairs and very 70s' sideboards, to the designers of today, such as Ron Arad, Gaetano Pesce and Philippe Starck.

Although it's located in a wing of the Louvre, the museum is independently run and the emphasis not on royal pieces. Instead, this place is all about French craftsmanship and design flair, tracking style trends and changing tastes over the centuries. Dotted around the collection are period rooms reconstructed whole, including Jeanne Lanvin's art deco suite, with its sultry blue boudoir and splendid marble bathroom. There's also a fabulous collection of jewellery, stunningly lit.

One side of the museum follows a chronological route, the other takes an interesting thematic approach, imaginatively mixing periods and bringing in items from the advertising and fashion museums also on the premises.

The museum has an excellent boutique, where you can find reproductions of historic dinner services. The smart modern restaurant, **Le Saut de Loup**, or 'wolf's leap', is named after the dry ditch that once ran along here as part of the Louvre's defenses.

*Musée des Arts Décoratifs; 107 rue de Rivoli; tel: 01 44 55 57 50; www.les artsdecoratifs.fr; Tue–Sun 11am–6pm; charge; map D2*

# Surrender your senses to **designer scents** by Serge Lutens, L'Artisan Parfumeur and Francis Kurkdjian

Perfume is a rarefied experience in **Les Salons du Palais-Royal Shiseido** (*pictured*; 142 Galerie de Vallois, Jardins du Palais-Royal; tel: 01 49 27 09 09; www.sergelutens. com; map E3), where you are led into an exquisite, purple-panelled boudoir to discover Serge Lutens's intense, sensual perfumes, presented in pretty bell-jar bottles. At the pristine white and zinc **Maison Francis Kurkdjian** (5 rue d'Alger; tel: 01 42 60 07 07; www.franciskurkdjian. com; map C3), near the Tuileries, Francis Kurkdjian takes a far more iconoclastic approach. He can create exclusive bespoke perfumes, but wants fragrance to be part of everyday life. Here you'll find not only men's and women's perfumes but also scented washing liquid and tubes of pear, herb, mint or violet liquid for blowing bubbles – meant for kids, adored by parents.

Opposite the Louvre, **L'Artisan Parfumeur** (2 rue de l'Amiral de Coligny; tel: 01 44 88 27 50; www. artisanparfumeur.com; map F1) is classic and elegant. Staff will take you through the huge range of perfumes, including bestseller Mûre et Musc, all made from natural ingredients. The approach here is very welcoming, with an atelier, where you can learn about scents or even concoct your own.

## OTHER SPECIALIST PERFUMERIES

**Détaille** (10 rue St-Lazare; tel: 01 48 78 68 50; www.detaille.com; map p82 E2): just as it was when founded in 1905, with colognes for Aéroplane, Yachting or Escrimeur.

**Diptyque** (34 boulevard St-Germain; tel: 01 43 26 77 44; www. diptyqueparis.fr; map p112 E4): for legendary room candles.

**Editions du Parfum Frédéric Malle** (37 rue de Grenelle; tel: 01 42 22 76 40; www.fredericmalle.com; map p132 D5): scents by famous noses and glass booths for sniffing them in.

**Etat Libre d'Orange** (69 rue des Archives; tel: 01 42 78 30 09; www. etatlibredorange.com; map p25 D6): cheerfully irreverent, great scents with silly names.

**Guerlain** (68 av des Champs-Elysées; tel: 01 45 62 52 57; www. guerlain.com; map p67 E4): the belle époque home of *Shalimar*, plus a beauty salon.

# Nose out next year's **fashion and lifestyle trends** on **rue St-Honoré**

Dignified rue St-Honoré (map C3-D3) has been a must for the dedicated shopper ever since pioneering concept store **Colette** (*pictured*; 213 rue St-Honoré; www.colette.fr) opened in 1998, conveniently close for the fashion and film set at black fronted **Hôtel Costes** (No. 239; tel: 01 42 44 50 00; www.hotelcostes.com) up the street. The white, minimalist, multi-level boutique takes the bazaar-like ethos of the department store and pares it down to a cutting-edge *what's next* in fashion, electronic gadgets, style magazines, make up, household objects and even toys. A decade on, it remains resolutely cool yet eclectic enough to spring a few surprises.

Okay, you wouldn't want to own everything here; and some of the limited edition trainers are absurdly expensive, strictly for the cognoscenti. But Colette has proved to have its finger on the pulse, the first to highlight some bright young designers such as Olympia Le Tan, with her clever little handbags made from classic bookcovers.

The mezzanine level exhibits hip photographers and graphic designers, while the basement bar is a fashionable lunch spot, specialising in… well, water,

mineral waters from all over the globe to be precise.

The arrival of Colette prompted a stream of French and Italian fashion labels to follow, including Roberto Cavalli, Miu Miu, Paule Ka, MaxMara, Jacques Le Corre's hats, and rising brands Sandro and Maje. At No. 173, the seductively wonky, glazed white earthenware teapots and dinner services of **Astier de Villatte** (tel: 01 42 60 74 13) evoke the shabby-chic château lifestyle of a lost aristocratic past. A true survivor is **Goyard** at No. 233, maker of luxury fitted trunks and luggage since 1825. And if you don't want water chez Colette, master *chocolatier* **Jean-Paul Hévin** (No. 231) has a cocoa-coloured Chocolate Bar tucked upstairs, for indulging in gâteaux and hot chocolate.

# Switch from **funfairs to Monet's waterlilies** all in the space of the **Tuileries gardens**

If variety is the spice of life, then the Tuileries gardens do pretty well. The park was originally laid out by Louis XIV's master gardener, André Le Nôtre, as part of the royal masterplan, stretching between the Louvre and the Tuileries palace on the site of an old tile (*tuile*) factory. At first sight, it looks very much the classic French park with long gravel paths, clipped geometric trees and white marble statuary; but it also contains kids' trampolines, a funky vegetable garden, and a line of cafés down the central axis.

The park makes for a good rest stop while visiting the Louvre but actually, can lay claim to plenty of art of its own. In the Jardin du Carrousel, near the Louvre, statues by Aristide Maillol hide between little hedges. Towards place de la Concorde, the **Jeu de Paume**, once a real tennis court, is used for photography exhibitions. The **Musée de l'Orangerie** provides the setting for Monet's fabulous later paintings of waterlilies. Two specially conceived oval rooms with softly filtered daylight allows you to appreciate the large curved canvases (the longest is 17 metres/yds long) of his water garden at Giverny, painted in different seasons and at different times of day between 1914 and 1926 and verging on abstraction. In the basement are Impressionist and post-Impressionist paintings collected by art dealer Paul Guillaume, notably Cézanne still lifes, early Matisse, and works by Soutine and Henri Rousseau.

*Jeu de Paume; 1 place de la Concorde; tel: 01 47 03 12 50; www.jeudepaume. org; Tue noon-9pm, Wed-Fri noon-7pm, Sat, Sun 10am-7pm; charge; map B3 Musée de l'Orangerie; Jardin des Tuileries; tel: 01 44 77 80 07; www. musee-orangerie.fr; Wed-Mon 9am-6pm; charge; map B3*

# Find traces of Paris's market past at **Les Halles**

For centuries Les Halles was the market heart, or perhaps belly, of Paris. It lost its soul when the wholesale market moved out of town in 1969 and the green metal pavilions were knocked down. The Forum des Halles (*pictured*; map G2) shopping centre and transport intersection that replaced it is largely a place to avoid; but traces of the area's lively market past do linger in the all-night restaurants that once fed market workers at all hours, and in the kitchen emporiums – such as **E Dehellerin** (18-20 rue Coquillière; tel: 01 42 36 53 13; www.e-dehillerin.fr; map F3), supplying chefs and keen amateur cooks for nearly two centuries.

South of the gardens, **La Tour Monthlhéry** (5 rue des Prouvaires; tel: 01 45 36 21 82; closed at weekends; map F2), aka Chez Denise, serves vast steaks and piles of lamb chops, 24 hours a day. It's dead trad and very popular with visitors, while **Le Bistrot des Halles** (15 rue des Halles; tel: 01 42 36 91 69; map G2), with its plate glass and formica, is a pleasantly un-dressed up spot for good, solid food and wines by the glass that is busy at lunchtime.

The end of the market is depicted in a charming relief, *The Departure of the Fruits and Vegetables from the Heart of Paris, 28 February 1969* by Raymond Mason inside **Eglise St-Eustache** (map G2), long the market church (also known for its impressive organ, with free recitals every Sunday at 5.30pm). Happily there are signs of improvement at the Forum des Halles. The gardens between the Forum and the Bourse du Commerce are being replanted and work has begun on **La Canopée**, an undulating glass and steel roof that will engulf the Forum like a giant ray, adding a library and concert hall to the shopping mall.

# Bask in romance and splendour at **Palais Garnier**

It's hard to imagine anything more extravagant than **Palais Garnier**, the opera house that has come to symbolise Second Empire Paris and Napoleon III's ambition to make Paris the most beautiful city in the world, and which is still an incredibly glamorous place to watch opera or the ballet. It was built between 1860 and 1875, after Charles Garnier saw off 170 competing architects, concocting a gloriously eclectic affair. If you don't have tickets for a performance, visit during the day to absorb the fabulously over-the-top decor. For visits, the entrance is at the side, beneath the ramp intended as an imperial carriage entrance, which gives the impression of walking through a grotto before you arrive at the grand staircase built in gaudy polychrome marble. Halfway up, two grandiose caryatids support the entrance to the Amphithéâtre (dress circle), where you can visit a *baignoire* (box) all in red damask and velvet and gaze over the auditorium with its massive chandelier and ceiling painted by Chagall, a controversial addition in 1964. Most opulent of all is the beautifully restored Grand Foyer, laden with marble and sculpted, gilded and painted ceilings that make even Versailles look modest.

The Palais Garnier recently added **L'Opéra**, a space-age red and white restaurant designed by architect Odile Decq, apparently just where Garnier had planned one. If you want to dine in true Garnier surroundings, Garnier also designed the opulent and very expensive **Café de la Paix** (5 place de l'Opéra; tel: 01 40 07 36 36; www.cafedelapaix.fr) across the square.

*Palais Garnier; place de l'Opéra; tel: 08 92 89 92 90; www.operadeparis.fr; performances Sept–July, visits daily 10am–5pm, mid-July–Aug until 6pm, 10am–1pm on matinée days; charge; map D5*

# Go behind the screen at the **Grand Rex**, an **art deco cinema** with an unusual tour

Inaugurated in front of 3,300 guests in 1932, **Le Grand Rex** is a temple to cinema and a masterpiece of Art Deco style, with its illuminated crown standing out like a beacon against the Paris skyline. French architect Auguste Bluysen and American John Eberson created a fantastical interior perfect for celluloid fantasies, mixing Spanish hacienda, palm trees, Mauresque minarets and classical pediments under a starry ceiling. You can still see films here today, along with rock concerts and special events; but to truly appreciate the building – and the art of cinema – take the clever, and very entertaining, 50-minute interactive **Les Etoiles du Rex** tour. The tour leads you into the projection room and literally behind the screen, letting you into the secrets of sound dubbing, storms and other tricks of the trade and with the chance to ham it up in *King Kong*. And in keeping with the best cinema tradition – there's a neat twist at the end.

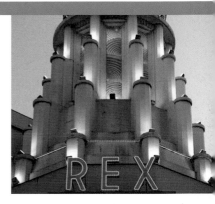

The Grands Boulevards are also where you'll find the heart of popular theatreland – or what the French call *théâtre des boulevards*, commercial theatre as opposed to public subsidised venues. Much of it resides in fanciful buildings such as the Théâtre de la Porte St-Martin, Théâtre du Gymnase, Théâtre des Variétés, Théatre des Nouveautés, and Théâtre de la Renaissance, where many plays and operas, for instance Offenbach's *La Belle Hélène*, were premiered in the 19th century.

A recent success is the **Comedy Club**, opened by comedian/actor/ entrepreneur Jamel Debbouze, for talent-spotting a multicultural line-up of up-and-coming comedians.

*Le Grand Rex; 1 boulevard Poissonnière; tel: 08 92 68 05 96; www. legrandrex.com; Les Etoiles du Rex tour, school holidays daily 10am–7pm, rest of year Wed–Sun, available in French or English; charge; map G4*
*Comedy Club; 42 boulevard Bonne Nouvelle; tel: 01 73 54 17 00; www.le comedyclub.fr; charge; map H4*

# Explore the network of **covered Passages** between Palais-Royal and Opéra

Like a cross between Oriental souk and cabinet of curiosities, the 19th-century covered passages were forerunners of the shopping mall or department stores, allowing Parisians to inspect novelties and traverse the town sheltered from the rain and horse-drawn traffic. Several still criss-cross the area between Palais-Royal and Opéra.

**Galerie Vivienne** (4 rue des Petits-Champs/6 rue Vivienne; map F3), inaugurated in 1826, is definitely the smartest of the passages (an aspiration revealed in the tag 'Galerie' rather than 'Passage'), with anchors and cornucopias carved on the wooden facades, fanlights and elaborate mosaic floors. Wine merchant **Legrand Filles et Fils** (tel: 01 42 60 07 12), with a huge choice of wines and a tasting counter on the spot, and popular **Bistrot Vivienne** (tel: 01 49 27 00 50) frame the entrance on rue des Petits-Champs; then come shawls and silks at **Wolff et Descourtis**, extravagantly cut couture at **Jean-Paul Gaultier**, upmarket *dépôt-vente* (consignment store) **La Marcelle**, colourful dresses at **Nathalie Garçon**, and the ladylike tea room **A Priori Thé** (tel: 01 42 97 48 75).

Along the street, **Passage Choiseul** (40 rue des Petits-Champs/ 23 rue St-Augustin) is shabbier, with cheap snack stalls, drycleaners and shoe shops – an interloper in this smart banking territory, although garlands of lights give it a jaunty air. This is where writer

## DROUOT THE AUCTIONEERS

Housed in a spiky modern building, **Drouot**, Paris's historic auction house, is a unique institution belonging to 111 *commissaire-priseurs* – specialist auctioneer-valuers – who hold thousands of sales here a year. Unlike the rather stuffy ambience of Sotheby's and Christie's, whose Paris branches are located in the *beaux quartiers* near avenue Matignon, the atmosphere at Drouot is wonderfully frantic. Dealers crowd around the catalogue counter before going up the escalators to the 18 salesrooms, where sales generally take place in the afternoon and viewings are held in the morning and the day before. Goods are fantastically eclectic, with quality and prices varying widely. This is the sort of place you come to with the full intention to view period furniture, 19th-century paintings, early photography or modern art... and find yourself looking in on an auction of Oriental antiquities, jewellery and watches, or fine wines.
*Drouot, 9 rue Drouot; tel: 01 48 00 20 20; www.drouot.com; Mon–Sat 11am–6pm, closed mid-Jul–mid-Sept; map F5*

Céline, whose mother was a lacemaker, grew up in the 1890s, depicted as the gloomy Passage des Beresinas in *Mort à Crédit*.

**Passage des Panoramas** (11 boulevard Montmartre/10 rue St-Marc) is the earliest of the covered passages. Today it's been colonised by wine bars, bistros, North African and Indian restaurants, including hip wine bar **Coinstot**, gourmet **Passage 53**, and old-fashioned **Bar des Variétés**, with old Paris Match covers glued over the bar.

Directly across the boulevard, **Passage Jouffroy** (10–12 boulevard Montmartre/9 rue de la Grange-Batalière) still most resembles a cabinet of curiosities, with **Grévin** (tel: 01 47 70 85 05; www.grevin.com), the Paris waxworks, on one side, **Café Zéphyr** – one of the few

to still have a billiards table – on the other, and the entrance to old-fashioned budget **Hôtel Chopin** halfway down. Eclectic treasures include walking sticks and curios at **M G Segas**, traditional toys and dolls' house furniture at both **Pain d'Epice** and **La Boite à Joujoux**, comic books and gems.

Across rue de la Grange-Batalière, **Passage Verdeau** (56 rue de la Grange-Batalière/31bis rue du Fbg-Montmartre) is almost entirely given over to antiques and antiquarian bookshops, and print and picture dealers, in an overflow from the Quartier Drouot (*see box*). Italian treats are to be had at deli **i Golosi**.

*Most passages Mon–Sat, around 8am–8pm; map E4-F5*

# Worship **food and classicism** at the **Madeleine**: luxury delis and a showbiz church

The **Eglise de la Madeleine** is about as close as you get to a Roman temple in Paris, a scaled-up version of the Maison Carrée in Nîmes with its colonnaded exterior atop a flight of steps. The foundation stone was laid in 1763 by Louis XV who wanted a showpiece basilica to fill the view from place de la Concorde. After failing to become either a library, bank or opera house during the Revolution, Napoleon plumped for a brash temple to the glory of his Grand Army. With the restoration of the monarchy, the plans reverted to those for a church but Pierre Vignon's temple design was kept. In 1842, the Eglise de la Madeleine was finally consecrated, 80 years after it was begun. The massive bronze doors are modelled on the baptistry doors in Florence, with reliefs depicting the Ten Commandments. Inside is a feast of florid pink, beige and blue marble, gilded friezes, coffered domes and pedimented side altars whose sculptures look far more like Roman generals than religious saints. Napoleon gets a look in too, holding centre stage in a vast mural of the history of Christianity in the half-dome behind the altar.

In the square outside, you can't help feeling, however, that the

true French religion holds sway. Promenade around the square to worship picturesque gâteaux and *traiteur* (caterer) treats at **Fauchon** (Nos. 24–26, 30; tel: 01 70 39 38 00), with its pink and black shopfronts and gold-plated bakery; fruit sculptures, jams and spices at **Hédiard** (No. 21; tel: 01 43 12 88 88); truffle-flavoured everythings at the **Maison de la Truffe** (No. 19; tel: 01 42 65 53 22), mustard at **Maille** (No. 6; tel: 01 40 15 06 00) and caviar at **Caviar Kaspia** (No. 17; tel: 01 42 65 33 32) and **Maison Prunier** (No. 15; tel: 01 47 42 98 98).

*Place de la Madeleine; map B4*

# Experience mealtimes in an old workers' canteen at legendary *bouillon* Chartier

Be prepared to queue and to share tables. A meal at **Chartier** is an experience: a rare surviving example of a *bouillon*, originally a sort of workers' canteen serving soup and stews to hungry workers. Chartier has kept its historic 1890s dining hall with high ceiling, tall mirrors, globe lights and varnished wooden booths, where you might find yourself sharing a table with nostalgics, impoverished Parisians or out-of-towners in search of a bargain. The waiters in long white aprons are a whirlwind of speed, with an incredible capacity for memorising orders and manipulating vast stacks of plates. The food is simple, sustaining and unbelievably cheap, from starters as basic as grated carrot for just €1.90, via decent main courses to a splurge on Mont Blanc (chestnut puree and whipped cream). You're not expected to linger, but before you leave, spot the numbered boxes once allocated to regulars to store their napkins.

*Chartier; 7 rue du Faubourg-Montmartre; tel: 01 47 70 86 29; www.restaurant-chartier.com; daily L and D; map F5*

---

**BEAUTIFUL BOUILLONS**

Two other former members of the Chartier chain survive, both with lovely listed art nouveau interiors: **Bouillon Racine** (3 rue Racine, 6th; tel: 01 44 32 15 60), and **Le Montparnasse 1900** (59 boulevard du Montparnasse, 6th; tel: 01 45 49 19 00), now serving more upmarket, classic brasserie food. Remaining more in the *bouillon* spirit is the vast three-storey **Café du Commerce** (51 rue du Commerce, 15th; tel: 01 45 75 03 27), opened in 1921 to feed Citroën car workers.

# **Shop till you drop** at the *grands magasins*, Galeries Lafayette and Printemps

On boulevard Haussmann, Galeries Lafayette, the world's largest department store, and neighbouring rival Printemps, famed for its colossal beauty floor, have been battling it out for over a century. Opened in 1893, **Galeries Lafayette** *(pictured)* likes to think it has everything and while it eternally modernises, here and there it still has the feel of an enormous bazaar, a wedding cake of commerce under the huge iron and stained glass dome. Fashion labels run from high-street fashion to luxury tags, the basement claims to be the largest shoe shop in the world and there are over 20 places to eat should you decide you want to spend your life here. Some things could only exist in France, such as the Bordeauxthèque, a temple to Bordeaux wines encompassing an inner circle of mythic vintage grands crus.

Behind its famous corner rotundas, its name picked out in floral mosaics, neighbouring **Printemps**, founded in 1865, has always seen itself as a leader in modernity – the first store to install electricity and fixed prices. Recently it has zapped bling into its gleaming white marble world of luxury, with a ground floor of mini boutiques for luxury shoes and accessories and a first floor of upper-crust jewellery and watches.

In summer, both stores open 'secret' rooftop restaurants with astonishing views.

*Galeries Lafayette; 40 boulevard Haussmann; tel: 01 42 82 34 56; www.galerieslafayette.com; Mon–Sat 9.30am–8pm, Thur until 9pm; map D5 Printemps; 64 boulevard Haussmann; tel: 01 42 82 50 00; www.printemps.com; Mon–Sat 9.30am–8pm, Thur until 10pm; map C5*

Find **Little Japan** on your doorstep: sushi, sashimi and even *shaba shaba* on **rue Ste-Anne**

Rue Ste-Anne, between Opéra and Palais Royal, represents the heart of Little Japan, lined with a diverse mix of restaurants, snack bars and canteens, and busy every lunchtime with office workers and Japanese expats. Here, as well as sushi and sashimi, you'll find noodle bars and less-familiar specialities such as *okonomiyaki* (a type of pancake).

The noodles at **Kunitoraya** (No. 39; tel: 01 47 03 33 65; www. kunitoraya.com) are so good the queues snake out into the street. Kunitoraya's speciality is thick, home-made, springy *udon* noodles, served in bowls of boiling hot broth – try the version with prawn tempura – or cold with various sauces. Aim to sit on the ground floor if possible, where there are stools around the counter and along the window. Minuscule **Michi** (No. 58 bis; tel: 01 40 20 49 93) is popular for good-value, freshly prepared sushi and sashimi, served around the counter with a view of the chef or in a tiny cellar.

For a more formal meal, **Bizan** (No. 56; tel: 01 42 96 67 76; www. isse-et-cie.fr) has a reputation for its Kyoto-style cuisine, by a chef who has worked for the Japanese royal family, served up in a very zen, pale-wood setting. Attractive stone-walled **Koetsu** (No. 42; tel: 01 40 15 99 90) offers excellent sushi and a wide range of other dishes, including grilled fish and beef teriyaki, while being one of those rare places where you'll find *shaba shaba*, an expensive but convivial Japanese 'fondue' whereby you dip finely sliced meat and vegetables into a pot of boiling broth.

Finally, nearby **Izakaya Issé** (45 rue de Richelieu; tel: 01 42 96 26 60; www.isse-et-cie.fr), a new 'bistro à sake', adapts Japanese food and sake to tapas-style snacking in a distressed decor of exposed stone and graffiti – a sign that a few restaurants are beginning to break out of the mould.

*Rue Ste-Anne; map E3–4*

# Champs-Elysées and Monceau

Champs-Elysées
and Monceau

0  100  200  300  400  500 m

0  100  200  300  400  500 yds

# Get into the spirit of 1900 at the **Grand Palais**, **Petit Palais** and **Pont Alexandre III**

The grand triumvirate put up for the Exposition Universelle of 1900 still captures the glitter of the belle époque and the optimism of the new century, showcasing all that was new in arts, technology and industry.

A bravura exercise in steel, glass and stone, with the largest glass roof in Europe, crowned by two bronze ensembles of galloping horses, the **Grand Palais** (www.grandpalais.fr; map F3) exudes belle époque confidence in its sheer size, wealth of decoration and unselfconsciously eclectic mix of styles – Classical motifs here, Art Nouveau flourishes there – perhaps not surprising as, after 260 architects entered the competition in 1896, its three facades were actually designed by three different architects,

Henri Deglane, Albert Louvet and Albert Thomas. Around 50 million visitors flocked to the fair in 1900. Later, the **Grand Nave** (avenue Winston Churchill) was used for artistic salons, motor shows and domestic appliance fairs. During World War II, it housed Nazi tanks; in 1994 it closed overnight when a metal beam fell off the roof, reopening only in 2005. It now houses all manner of events and salons, from the giant art installations of Monumenta (Kiefer, Serra, Boltanski and Kapoor, so far), to exclusive fashion shows and showjumping. The avenue Eisenhower wing contains the **Galeries Nationales** (tel: 01 44 13 17 17) used for prestigious, crowd-pulling art exhibitions, and the avenue Franklin Roosevelt wing contains the old-fashioned

**Palais de la Découverte** (tel: 01 56 43 20 20; www.palais-decouverte.fr) science museum.

Crown your visit with a meal, or the luxury snacks served all afternoon, at **Mini Palais** (tel: 01 42 56 42 46; www.minipalais. fr), the Grand Palais's glamorous restaurant decorated to resemble a 19th-century artist's studio.

Although the Grand Palais grabs most of the attention, the **Petit Palais** (tel: 01 53 43 40 00; www.petitpalais.paris.fr; map G3) across the street is another fanciful confection of coloured marble, mosaics and wrought iron. Today, many people come here for the temporary exhibitions, but the eclectic fine art collection of the Ville de Paris offers plenty of discoveries: works by Bonnard and Cézanne and a gallery of showstopper art nouveau vases made for the Great Exhibition.

> **1900 FEVER**
> A few other buildings survive from the enthusiasm for all things 1900: Le Train Bleu, the opulent brasserie inside Gare de Lyon, beautiful Art Nouveau Brasserie Julien and, of course, Gare d'Orsay, no longer a train station.

The most surprising part of the ensemble? Probably, **Pont Alexandre III** built as a link to Les Invalides across the Seine – with a cacophony of ships and dolphins, trident-bearing cherubs and fancy lampposts with lion's paws – whose name, at the time, some disliked for its association with imperial Russia. You can even go inside the bridge, where venue the **Showcase** (under Pont Alexandre III, Port des Champs-Elysées; tel: 01 45 61 25 43; www.showcase.fr; map G2) hosts bands and DJs at weekends in secret rooms with watery views.

# Window shop on **avenue Montaigne** and **Faubourg-St-Honoré**

The mere mention of Avenue Montaigne evokes the mythic world of haute-couture. The luxurious *Triangle d'Or* (golden triangle) formed by avenues Montaigne, George V and rue François 1er is a world away from the nearby Champs-Elysées. Couture and upmarket ready-to-wear labels provide impressive window-shopping, the impression of exclusivity often reinforced by the setting – aristocratic houses set back behind iron railings.

On avenue Montaigne, you'll find the distinctive pearl-grey facade of **Dior** (No. 30), where Christian Dior revolutionised fashion with the New Look in 1957, along with classic houses **Ungaro** (No. 2), **Nina Ricci** (No. 39), **Valentino** (No. 17), **Chanel** (No. 42), **Chloé** (No. 44) and **Céline** (No. 36), and Italians **Prada** (No. 10) and **Giorgio Armani** (No. 18). Nearby, there's **Balenciaga** (10 avenue George V), back at the top with superb cuts and beautiful leatherware designed by Nicolas Ghesquière, and **Balmain** (44 rue François 1er). At lunchtime, the sunglasses set hangs out at **L'Avenue** (No. 41; tel: 01 40 70 14 91), the fashionable Costes brasserie, while at night, they survey the city from **La Maison Blanche** (No. 15; tel: 01 47 23 55 99; www.maison-blanche.fr), the modern eatery perched atop the Théâtre des Champs-Elysées.

There's a second designer fashion nucleus on the other side of the Champs-Elysées along **rue du Faubourg-St-Honoré**, where upmarket French and Italian labels follow in the footsteps of **Lanvin** at No. 22. Here Jeanne Lanvin set up as a *modiste* in 1889, later one of the first designers to introduce sportswear and perfume lines in the 1920s. No. 22 is now the womenswear shop, while the menswear boutique at No. 15 still has some of its 1920s art deco furniture by Albert Rateau.

*Triangle d'Or; map E3*
*Rue du Faubourg-St Honoré; map G-H3*

# Dine with the powerbrokers at ministerial favourites **Laurent** and **Lasserre**

Conveniently close to the Elysées palace and the Ministry of the Interior, salmon-coloured **Laurent** (41 avenue Gabriel; tel: 01 42 25 00 39; www.le-laurent.com; map F3) is particularly splendid in summer when dining is under parasols bordering the Champs-Elysées gardens, yet discretely shielded from the hoi polloi. The food is wonderful (President Sarkozy apparently always has lobster salad), and the outdoor setting makes it one of the most relaxed of Paris's top restaurants.

Similarly, although international foodies flock to Alain Ducasse at the Plaza Athénée, when it comes to a business lunch you're more likely to catch politicians, and media and business magnates discussing strategy in **Le Relais Plaza** (21 avenue Montaigne; tel: 01 53 67 64 00; www. plaza-athenee-paris. com; map E3), its adjoining, slightly more casual, Art Deco brasserie.

**Lasserre** (17 avenue Franklin Roosevelt; tel: 01 43 59 02 13; www.restaurant-lasserre.com; map F3) is a legend for its *pigeon Malraux* (pigeon stuffed with foie gras), created for then-minister of culture André Malraux who lunched here every day in the 1960s, and the retractable roof. An almost unbelievable number of staff hover with trays and bottles, but the restaurant has recently had an injection of energy with the arrival of chef Christophe Moret.

At sleek modern **Le Chiberta** (3 rue Arsène Houssaye; tel: 01 53 53 42 00; www.lechirberta.com; map D4), you can dine amid modern art or at the bar. Run by Guy Savoy, star turns from his gastronomic restaurant include grapefruit terrine with Earl Grey sauce.

If you do one three star, perhaps make it **Pierre Gagnaire** (6 rue Balzac; tel: 01 58 36 12 50; www.pierre-gagnaire. com; map E4), where the relatively affordable business lunch menu gives an insight into Gagnaire's light, fabulously inventive cuisine.

# Have tea with Tiepolo at **Musée Jacquemart-André**

A Tiepolo in the tea room is just a hint of the grand lifestyle and superb artworks amassed by a couple of fervent art collectors.

Edouard André, scion of a rich banking family, and his artist wife Nélie Jacquemart built this grand mansion in 1869-75 to house the collection they had picked up on their travels or unearthed in auction houses. It gives a vision of grand 19th-century living, with its galleried music room – where the couple hosted concerts and balls – Moorish-style smoking room, hung with English portraits, winter garden with pot plants, and the extravagant double staircase, decorated with a grand fresco by Tiepolo, originally painted for the Villa Contarini. Upstairs, Nelie's former studio became their 'Italian museum' whose treasures include a small Botticelli, Uccello's jewel-like *St George and the Dragon*, and glazed terracotta reliefs by the della Robbia family.

The museum reflects the magpie, eclectic eye of these collectors but also their impeccable taste. Even the 18th-century portraits, now often seen as dull and pompous are of exceptional quality, for instance a charming portrait by Nattier of the *Mathilde de Canisy*, with a garland of flowers

and a shimmery satin dress, and Elizabeth Vigée-Lebrun's luminous *Countess Catherine Skavronskaia*. In the library, Dutch paintings include Rembrandt's *The Pilgrims of Emmaus*, the small canvas illuminated by a shaft of light.

As to tea with Tiepolo: the former dining room is now an elegant café and salon de thé, its walls hung with tapestries and Tiepolo resplendent on the ceiling.

*Musée Jacquemart-André; 158 boulevard Haussmann; tel: 01 45 62 11 59; www.musee-jacquemart-andre.com; daily 10am–6pm; charge; map F5*

# Go on a mini tour of France at the **Cité de l'Architecture**

Medieval monuments and modern architecture give an intriguing double identity to the **Cité de l'Architecture**, born in 2007. The sweeping ground-floor gallery is like a mini tour of France via the doorways and past sculpted pinacles of a hit list of Romanesque and Gothic churches. Full-size reproductions of the Last Judgement from the church at Conques, the medieval tomb of the Dukes of Burgundy and 300 others add up to a tour de force of plaster casting. On the first floor, there's a dim succession of mysterious frescoed church interiors before the second floor leaps into the mid 19th century and modernity, with iron structures and skyscrapers, architectural maquettes, film archives, Paris's circular Maison de la Radio and a spectacular full-size mock-up of one of the duplex apartments in Le Corbusier's Cité

Radieuse, in Marseille. The Cité also puts on temporary exhibitions in huge basement galleries. More offbeat is the former director's apartment (weekends only), which the magazine *Elle Decoration* invites designers – such as Jean-Paul Gaultier – to decorate in a year-long installation. The museum's setting, the Palais de Chaillot, is itself a monument of imposing Modernist classical revival architecture put up for the world fair of 1937 and also home to the Musée de la Marine (maritime museum), the Musée de l'Homme (ethnology museum; closed until 2012) and the Théâtre National de Chaillot (theatre and dance).

*Cité de l'Architecture; Palais de Chaillot, 1 place du Trocadéro; tel: 01 58 51 52 00; www.citechaillot.fr; Mon, Wed, Fri–Sun 11am–7pm, Thur 11am–9pm; charge; map C2*

# See a **late night art** show at the **Palais de Tokyo**

If you're in the mood for adventurous art, check out what's on at contemporary art space the **Palais de Tokyo**. The art is international, experimental and often highly conceptual and you may feel you need a dose of theory to understand it; but the Palais does its best to make its shows accessible – gallery attendants are all trained mediators. Opened in 2001 in a vast modernist classical pavilion built for the 1937 International Exposition, the interior looks deliberately unfinished, which gives it a slightly underground appeal, especially at night when it's open until midnight. There's an art bookshop in a cage, trendy restaurant Tokyo Eat and the very cool BlackBlock gift shop, where eclectic items from inexpensive badges to artists' limited editions are shown in fridge cabinets. Additional galleries are set to open in the cavernous building come 2012.

During the day, the Palais de Tokyo can be combined with the **Musée d'Art Moderne de la Ville de Paris**, the municipal museum of modern art, which occupies the other wing. The permanent collection is strong on Cubism, Orphism, the Ecole de Paris, and works by Arp and Fautrier. Be sure to look at Raoul Dufy's vast mural *La Fée Electricité* (The Electricity Fairy). Painted for the 1937 electricity pavilion, it is a joyous celebration of electrical power and all those behind it, from Greek gods to Watt and Ampère.

*Palais de Tokyo; 13 avenue du Président-Wilson; tel: 01 47 23 54 01; www.palaisdetokyo.com; Tue–Sun noon–midnight, until 9pm during building work; charge; map D2*
*Musée d'Art Moderne de la Ville de Paris; 11 avenue du Président-Wilson; tel: 01 53 67 40 00; www.mam.paris.fr; Tue–Sun 10am–6pm; collection free, charge for temporary exhibitions; map D2*

Find reasons to **celebrate** on the **Champs-Elysées**, laid out as Napoleon's triumphal way

Much of the time it's hard to understand the fuss about the Champs-Elysées, automatically dubbed 'the most beautiful avenue in the world' by the French – but the Champs do come into their own for national celebrations, such as the military parade on *le Quatorze Juillet* (Bastille Day) and the finale of the Tour de France.

The Champs were first laid out as a promenade by royal gardener André Le Nôtre in an extension of the Tuileries gardens, later forming Napoleon's triumphal way to the Arc de Triomphe. The lower half near place de la Concorde still has a pleasure garden feel, with the pavilions of restaurants Ledoyen (map G3) and Laurent (*p.71*), and theatres Marigny and Rond-Point.

In the late 19th century, it became a fashionable residential street. A few traces of grandeur remain in the mansions of the Rond-Point des Champs-Elysées, the Hôtel de la Païva (No. 25), the original Guerlain perfume store (No. 68), Le Fouquet's brasserie (No. 97) and Louis Vuitton's glitzy flagship store at No. 101. At the top is the celebrated **Publicis Drugstore** (No. 133; www.publicisdrugstore.com) founded by advertising maestro Marcel Bleustein-Blanchet in the 1950s. It contains an upmarket deli, cigar shop, international newsagent, cinemas and the Atelier Etoile de Joël Robuchon (tel: 01 47 23 75 75). The high-concept car showrooms of Renault, Toyota and Citroën are a curious relic from when only the very rich could contemplate owning a vehicle.

At the western end, the **Arc de Triomphe** is another of Napoleon's showstoppers, modelled on the Arch of Titus in Rome but bigger, inaugurated in 1836 long after his downfall. A climb to the top rewards you with entrancing views of the traffic milling around below.

*Arc de Triomphe; place de l'Etoile (access by underpass); tel: 01 55 37 73 77; www.arc-de-triomphe.monuments-nationaux.fr, daily 10am–11pm, winter until 10.30pm; charge; map D4*

# Mix with the privileged *beau monde* at **Parc Monceau**

**Parc Monceau** was created in the 1770s by Philipe Egalité, Duc d'Orléans, brother of Louis XVI, who filled it with picturesque follies – a pyramid, an antique colonnade around the lake, a Venetian bridge over the stream – amid rolling lawns and magnificient trees. Ever-popular with the area's nannies and well-bred schoolchildren, the park is at the heart of a privileged residential district built up since the mid-19th century. Some put up mini French châteaux here (such as the Musée Jacquemart-André, *p.72*), others had more exotic tastes – witness the red lacquered chinoiserie house at 48 rue de Courcelles, built for an Oriental art dealer. Russian émigrés constructed **Alexandre Nevsky Russian Orthodox Cathedral** (12 rue Daru; tel: 01 42 27 37 24), with five towers topped by onion domes.

Overlooking the park, two of the fine mansions are now museums. The **Musée Nissim de Camondo** was erected in 1911 by Moïse de Camondo, a wealthy banker from Constantinople, in a style quite out of its time yet with all mod cons, who filled it with a fabulous collection of 18th-century decorative arts: Sèvres and Meissen porcelain, Aubusson carpets and Beauvais tapestries.

Another grand mansion belonged to banker and voyager Henri Cernuschi, a refugee Italian revolutionary who made a fortune in banking before touring Asia in 1871–2. A giant Japanese buddha and the Chinese pots he brought back formed the foundations of the **Musée Cernuschi**, which is particularly strong on Chinese ceramics and funerary figures.

*Musée Cernuschi; 7 avenue Vélasquez; tel: 01 53 96 21 50; www.paris.fr; Tue–Sun 1am–6pm; free; map F5*
*Musée Nissim de Camondo; 63 de Monceau; tel: 01 53 89 06 50; www.les artsdecoratifs.fr; Wed–Sun 10am–5.30pm; charge; map F5*
*Parc Monceau; 55 boulevard de Courcelles (other entrances on avenues Vélasquez, Van Dyck, Ruysdael); www. paris.fr; daily summer 7am–9/10pm, winter 7am–8pm; free; map F5*

# Atone for Louis XVI and Marie-Antoinette at the
## Chapelle Expiatoire

In a slightly forgotten corner between the Madeleine and boulevard Haussmann, the **Chapelle Expiatoire** is a small masterpiece of neoclassical architecture and one of the most moving reminders of the French Revolution. Located on the site of the former cemetery of the Madeleine, where the guillotined bodies of Louis XVI and Marie-Antoinette were thrown into a pit in 1793, the golden stone chapel was commissioned by restoration monarch Louis XVIII (brother of Louis XVI) and built 1816–26 by Fontaine, one of the architects of the rue de Rivoli for Napoleon.

A beautifully pared-back entrance pavilion hides the chapel itself, which is reached at the rear of a courtyard past stylised tombs in memory of the Swiss guards massacred when protecting the king and queen at the Tuileries palace in 1792. Inside the chapel, face to face, stand two white marble statues: Marie-Antoinette accompanied by Religion bearing a cross (by Cortot), and Louis XVI ascending to heaven with an angel (by Bosio).

The chapel long had a dubious reputation as a gathering point for reactionary royalists, and was even nearly demolished in the 1880s to make way for a station. But here, more so than at any other of the city's revolutionary sights, the calm and sobriety of the architecture combine to create something incredibly mournful and elegiac.

*Chapelle Expiatoire; Square Louis XVI, 29 rue Pasquier; tel: 01 44 32 18 00; www.chapelle-expiatoire.monuments-nationaux.fr; Thur–Sat 1–5pm; charge; map H4*

# Find your inner zen and a serene Japanese garden at **Musée Guimet** and the **Panthéon Bouddhique**

A seven-headed snake from Cambodia's Angkor Wat temple complex now provides a lead to the collection of beautifully poised Khmer sculptures which form the centrepiece of **Musée Guimet** (*pictured*), the national collection of Asian art. Here you really are in another, zen, world peopled by Hindu and Buddhist gods each more rounded and beatifically smiling than the last. Other highlights include Tibetan tantras and sculptures from Afghanistan.

While the main museum is beautifully displayed, with sober, uncluttered calm, the **Panthéon Bouddhique**, a few doors up the street, gives a better idea of Emile Guimet's original vision of a museum dedicated to religions and popular worship. Here, the ranks of bronze and painted wood gods, deities and sacred temple figures amassed on a journey to Japan in 1876 give the feel of an Oriental shrine, a journey extended by the bamboo and stepping stones in the small Japanese garden and the tea pavilion at the rear.

For a very chic place to eat, continue up to place des Etats-Unis. Here, glass manufacturer **Baccarat** has its splendid Parisian showrooms, museum gallery and the Cristal Room restaurant in rooms given a brilliantly tongue-in-cheek decor by Philippe Starck – with food overseen by Grand Véfour chef Guy Martin and magnificent chandeliers, naturally.

*Musée (National des Arts Asiatiques) Guimet; 6 place d'Iéna; tel: 01 56 52 53 00; www.guimet.fr; Wed–Sun 10am–6pm; charge; map D3*
*Panthéon Bouddhique; 19 avenue d'Iéna; tel: 01 40 73 88 00; www.guimet. fr; Wed–Mon 9.45am–5.45pm; free; map D3*
*Baccarat; 11 place des Etats-Unis; tel: 01 01 40 22 11 10; www.baccarat.fr; museum gallery Mon, Wed–Sat 10am–6pm; charge; restaurant L and D Mon–Sat; map D3*

# Have a sybaritic **chocolate wrap** at the luxury **George V spa**

Resembling a scene from Marie-Antoinette's Versailles (the Sofia Coppola version), The Spa at the **Four Seasons George V** is a sexy, soft-focus take on period grandeur, where Louis XVI chairs, misty landscapes and *toile de jouy* prints are the backdrop for all manner of treatments – with the bonus of a great pool. Its ultimate treat has to be the winter chocolate special, a skin-softening, energy-boosting package where you are pampered with a choc chip orange body scrub, sybaritic swiss chocolate wrap and finally cocoa bean oil for a deep chocolate massage.

Today's luxury hotels rival each other with ever more luxurious spas and both exotic and exclusive solutions to stress, jetlag and advancing age. At the **Hôtel Saint James** (*pictured*), it's stone age chic at the Gemology spa, harnessing minerals and trace elements found in precious and semi-precious stones for cosmetics, citrine and volcanic mud body scrubs and massages with rock crystal, quartz, and agate, all in a lovely Moorish interior of tiles and glass lamps.

The Anne Semonin Spa at **Le Bristol** is a soothing candlelit environment for a programme of anti-stress treatments, harnessing aromatherapy, cryotherapy, shiatsu and reflexology, accompanied by tea and macaroons.

A glowing white globe and silvery butterflies lead you into the spa at the **Mandarin Oriental**, with sumptuous treatment cabins lining the swimming pool. Signature treatments combine aromatherapy and Chinese herbal medicine.

*Four Seasons George V; 31 avenue George V; tel: 01 49 52 72 10; www.four seasons.com/paris; map E3*
*Hôtel Saint James; 43 avenue Bugeaud; tel: 01 44 05 81 81; www.saint-james-paris.com; map A4*
*Le Bristol; 108 rue du Faubourg-St-Honoré; tel: 01 42 66 24 22; www.lebristol paris.com; map G4*
*Mandarin Oriental; 251 rue St-Honoré; tel: 01 70 98 78 88; www.mandarin oriental.com; map p46 C3*

## Montmartre and Pigalle

# Walk through walls in hilly **Montmartre** and access quiet streets, pretty cottages and an ancient vineyard

A bronze head, hand and a trousered leg emerge strangely from a wall on place Marcel Aymé, a reference to Marcel Aymé's 1943 short story *Le Passe Muraille* about Dutilleul, a civil servant who discovers he can walk through walls. Using his skill to rob jewellers, he finally comes to a literally sticky end – stuck in the wall – pretty much where the sculpture is. Today, this perhaps serves as a good metaphor for exploring the area: once past overcrowded place du Tertre you'll find you can still slip into quiet, deserted streets, with picturesque cottages and artists'

studios, and take short cuts by steep stairways.

Place du Tertre is at the junction of rue Norvins, where Aymé lived, and avenue Junot, with its unusual houses, notably the **Maison Tristan Tzara** at No. 15, designed in 1926 by Austrian architect Adolphe Loos; and the **Hôtel Particulier** at No. 23 (tel: 01 53 41 81 40; www.hotel-particulier-montmartre.com), an exclusive five-room hotel entered off a stairway, past an overgrown lump of rock known as the witch's stone.

In the other direction, rue des Saules descends past the **Montmartre vineyard**, a relic of the vines that once covered the district. The grapes are harvested with much pomp every October and carried in a costumed procession to the town hall.

Overlooking the vines, the endearingly old-fashioned **Musée de Montmartre** occupies a manor house where Auguste Renoir rented a studio; a renovation programme is under way that will include replanting the gardens as they were when he painted them.

*Musée de Montmartre; 12 rue Cortot; tel: 01 49 25 89 37; www.museede montmartre.fr; daily 10am–6pm; charge; map E5*

Observe local characters in the **bars of Abbesses** – also officially home to the **best baguette** in Paris

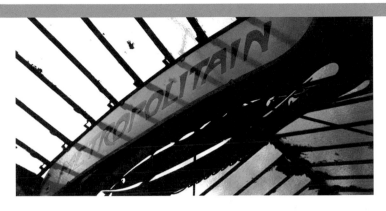

Part of Montmartre's appeal lies in its many facets. Just seconds from a tourist trap you can be in authentic, lived-in Paris or at a corner café packed with eclectic locals – and in Abbesses, arty types or a drag queen are equally likely.

Place des Abbesses has one of Paris's two métro stations still with its Art Nouveau glass canopy by Hector Guimard, and a small garden where a tiled wall reads '1 love you' in 300 languages. Across the square, take a look inside the curious church of **St-Jean-de-Montmartre**. Behind its brick facade studded with turquoise ceramics, the church built in 1894–1904 was a pioneer in the use of reinforced concrete.

Rue des Abbesses is sprinkled with good food shops, although its one-off clothes shops are slowly being replaced by chains.

Good places for a breather are busy bar **Le Sancerre** (No. 35; tel: 01 42 58 08 20); wine merchants **La Cave des Abbesses** (No. 43; tel: 01 42 52 81 54), with a few tables outside in summer and a tiny wine bar at the rear where you can try different wines, and there's a real fire in winter; and **La Marlotte** (No. 52; tel: 01 46 06 28 15), an old-fashioned brasserie that still draws a dedicated crowd of offbeat regulars for oysters and steaks.

There's clearly something in the hill air. Two bakers on the street have won the city's prize for the best baguette in Paris: Pascal Barillon at **Au Levain d'Antan** (No. 6) in 2011 and Djibril Bodian at **Le Grenier à Pain Abbesses** (No. 38).

*Abbesses; map E4*

# Visit Symbolist artist **Gustave Moreau** at his **home and studio**

With hundreds of paintings covering the walls and thousands of drawings and studies that you can pull out on wooden shutters, the double-storey studio of Symbolist artist Gustave Moreau (1826–98) constitutes one of the most captivating and eccentric museums in Paris, testimony to the artist's feverish creativity. Inspired by mythology and the Bible, Renaissance painting, the Orient and India, some of Moreau's pet subjects – such as lascivious Salome, or Oedipus and the Sphinx – appear again and again. There are centaurs, unicorns and other mystical beasts, fantastical architecture, mysterious caves and forests in dreamy works at once charged with detail and alternating with darker, broader patches pierced by intense spots of colour. Amid highly finished paintings you'll find works in progress, along with a case of unusual, red wax sculptures used as working models to plot out compositions. Although you can see Moreau's paintings in museums, here you get a true idea of his ferment of ideas and the artist's own vision of immortality.

During his lifetime, Moreau had planned for his studio to become a museum, transforming the building, which he left with all its contents to the state, and appointing his favourite pupil, the painter Georges Rouault, as first curator. Even the downstairs apartment was part of his schema. Although it looks every bit the image of cluttered 19th-century living, it was arranged symbolically by the artist as a sort of conceptual artwork in its own right.

*Musée National Gustave Moreau; 14 rue de la Rochefoucauld; tel: 01 48 74 38 50; www.musee-moreau.fr; Wed–Mon 10am–12.45pm, 2–5.15pm; charge; map D3*

# Admire the pathos at **Montmartre cemetery**

Originally gypsum quarries, then a gruesome mass grave for victims of the Revolution before becoming the city's new northern cemetery in 1825, today, the **Cimetière de Montmartre** is romantically overgrown, with rows of tombs and emotive sculptures of weeping nymphs, doom figures, distraught maidens, and an unlikely copy of Michelangelo's Moses.

Many of the people buried here are intrinsic to the artistic history of the area, among them society courtesan Alphonsine Plessis. Mistress first of Alexandre Dumas fils (son), later of Liszt and then the Comte of Perregaux, before dying of tuberculosis in 1847 aged just 23, she was the model for Marguerite Gautier in Dumas's *La Dame aux Camélias* and Violetta in Verdi's *La Traviata*.

Other graves include composers Jacques Offenbach and Hector Berlioz, artists Gustave Moreau (*p.86*) and Edgar Degas, in a family vault marked Famille de Gas, dancers Nijinsky – sculpted in bronze as Harlequin – and Louise Weber, alias the Moulin Rouge's La Goulue with an epitaph 'creatrice of the cancan', and new wave film director François Truffaut.

The most visited tomb of all is probably that of Dalida, stage name for Yolanda Gigliotti, Italo-Egyptian singer and gay icon, who committed suicide in 1987. Her dramatic tomb (on the terraces to the right of the entrance), portraying the singer in front of a triumphal arch and sunburst, is always strewn with flowers. You can also see the fanciful turreted house where she lived at 23 rue Orchampt, and a bronze bust on nearby place Dalida.

*Cimetière de Montmartre; 20 avenue Rachel; tel: 01 53 42 36 30; www.paris. fr, Mon-Fri 8am-6pm, Sat 8.30am-6pm, Sun 9am-6pm, closes 5.30pm in winter; free; map D5*

# Empathise with **the Romantics**: George Sand, Chopin and Ary Scheffer at the **Musée de la Vie Romantique**

A lock of hair, plaster casts of her and Frederic Chopin's hands, family portraits, watercolours, her great grandfather's snuffbox and desk create a gentle shrine to George Sand and Romanticism in the pretty green-shuttered house once belonging to Dutch-born artist Ary Scheffer. Nevertheless, the **Musée de la Vie Romantique** comes more in the spirit of romantic melancholia than sublime passion, and as such is surely far too prim for Sand – alias Amantine-Aurore Lucile Dupin, prolific novelist, playwright and journalist, bohemian, cigar smoker and liberated woman, who dared shock society by divorcing her husband and taking a succession of prominent lovers.

Upstairs you'll find portraits and historic paintings by Ary Scheffer,

a successful society portrait painter and friend of Napoleon, as well as other decidedly minor 19th-century artists. Scheffer's two high-ceilinged, north-facing studios across the courtyard are now used for exhibitions. A pleasant tea room opens in the garden conservatory during summer.

Scheffer was more inspiring as a host than as a painter, inviting the artists and intellectuals of the day to his salons and soirées. Delacroix (who taught drawing to Sand's son Maurice), Liszt, Rossini, Turgenev and Charles Dickens were all guests here, as well as Sand and Chopin.

*Musée de la Vie Romantique; 16 rue Chaptal, 75009; tel: 01 53 31 95 67; www.vie-romantique.paris.fr; Tue–Sun 10am–6pm; free; map D3*

## Discover **La Nouvelle Athènes**, including the house where Bizet is said to have penned *Carmen*

The Musée de la Vie Romantique *(opposite)* is a good starting point for exploring the district, which was an intellectual hub in the early 19th century, dubbed the Nouvelle Athènes for its colony of writers, artists, composers and actors, as well as *lorettes* – the lavishly dressed demi-mondaines who frequented the area around Notre-Dame-de-Lorette.

So where did George Sand actually live? She divided her time between the family home at Nohant in the Creuse and Paris, living in rue Pigalle before moving, in 1842, to **Square d'Orléans**. An elegant private garden square, designed in 1830 by English architect Edward Crecy, during the week you can nonetheless wander into it from 80 rue Taitbout. Lovers Sand and Chopin rented facing apartments at Nos 5 and 9 where she lived with her two children and Chopin had space to compose.

The area is peppered with fine private residences from the days before the 19th-century uniformisation of Paris by civic planner Georges-Eugène Haussmann – such as on place St-Georges, with its neo-Renaissance *hôtels particuliers*; on rue St-Lazare and rue Notre-Dame-de-Lorette, where Delacroix had a studio; or

at 26 rue de la Tour d'Auvergne, where Georges Bizet was born in 1838. The prettiest of the lot are on **rue de la Tour-des-Dames** – home to the famous actor Talma whose portrait was painted by Delacroix – and actresses Madame Mars, a star at the Comédie Française, who lived in the elegant villa at No. 1, and Mademoiselle Duchesnois, who lived in the unusual semi-circular No. 3. There's more Bizet at 22 rue de Douai/34 rue Duperré, where cocktail bar **Le Carmen** (tel: 01 45 26 50 00; map D4) now occupies the extravagant period salons, complete with mouldings and sculpted caryatids, of the house where Bizet is said to have written *Carmen*.

*Square d' Orléans; map E3*

# Survey the city from the **Sacré-Coeur**

The sugary white church of *Sacré-Coeur* is one of those buildings you suddenly glimpse in the distance from some of the most unlikely spots in Paris, partly because it stands on a hill, partly because it is built in travertine limestone that secretes calcite when it rains, keeping the stone perpetually white. It was built between 1875 and 1919 as an act of penance for France's defeat in the 1870 Franco-Prussian War and the succeeding Commune, caused, some believed, by a national lack of religion since the French Revolution. The church was paid for by public subscription, with donors' names carved in the stone, and located on the hill where Saint Denis was martyred in the 3rd century – hence 'martyr's mount' (Montmartre), although the name could also come from an even earlier temple to Mars that is thought to have stood here. Architect Paul Abadie designed the basilica in a Romano-Byzantine style with a clutter of domes and bronze equestrian statues of Joan of Arc and St Louis, two symbols of the French nation, over the portico. Inside it's gloriously kitsch, with a vast glittery mosaic in the apse, more mosaics in the side chapels and a huge vaulted crypt with statues of saints. If you've got the energy, you can climb up to the top of the dome, although the views are also pretty good from the parvis outside the church, with its tiers of steps, or from the gardens of square Wilmotte that meander round to the side. In keeping with Montmartre's belief that it is a mountain and not simply a hill, you can also reach the church by funicular (fare: one metro ticket).

*Basilica Sacré-Coeur-de-Montmartre; place du Parvis du Sacré-Coeur; www. sacre-coeur-montmartre.com; daily 6am–10.30pm, dome summer 9am–7pm, winter 9am–6pm, crypt times vary; charge for dome; map F5*

Catch a concert, an accordion fest or a cheeky drag show in the old **music halls of Pigalle**

Montmartre's past as a place for weekend entertainment lives on in a string of fanciful concert halls amid the peep shows and souvenir stalls of boulevard Rochechouart. **L'Elysée Montmartre** (No. 72; tel: 01 44 92 45 36), opened in 1807, is said to have seen the birth of the cancan. Now one of Paris's best spots for rock, roots and the long-running Sunday *Bal*, it has an ornate facade that's listed, but the roof was damaged in a fire in 2011 and when the venue will reopen is still undecided. A few doors away is the **Théâtre du Trianon** (No. 80; tel: 01 44 92 78 00), an old operetta and vaudeville hall now used for foot-stomping musicals and accordion fests, as well as rock and *chanson*. It recently reopened **Le Petit Trianon** (tel: 01 44 92 78 08), its lovely vintage café-bistro downstairs. **La Cigale** (No. 120; tel:

01 49 25 81 75) is another glorious old venue with an art deco facade and tiered balcony, while next door, laidback café **La Fourmi** (74 rue des Martyrs; tel: 01 42 64 70 35) is popular before gigs or clubbing at **Le Divan du Monde** (75 rue des Martyrs; tel: 01 42 52 02 46), a sultry club that has succeeded the Divan Japanais, immortalised in posters by Toulouse-Lautrec.

As to the famous **Moulin Rouge** (82 boulevard de Clichy; tel: 01 53 09 82 82), it largely plays to coachloads of tourists. For a more fun alternative, try **Chez Michou** (80 rue des Martyrs; tel: 01 46 06 16 04), where dapper, blue-jacketed Michou comperes a cheeky drag show with a cast of glittering divas.

*Pigalle; map D-F4*

# Live like a modern bohemian in **SoPi**

What was yesterday's bohemian neighbourhood has become the habitat of the modern 'bobo' or *bourgeois bohème* – though today she is more likely to be eating cheesecake and pushing a buggy than starving in a garret. Climbing like a spine through burgeoning SoPi (southern Pigalle, south of boulevards de Clichy and Rochechouart as opposed to NoPi, on the flanks of Montmartre) is rue des Martyrs. Its lower reaches, pedestrianised on Sunday mornings, are packed with food shops: a *fromagerie* specialising in goat's cheese, a Greek deli, Italian restaurant **Fuxia**

and its grocery offshoot, olive oil emporium **Première Pression Provence** (No. 9), **Aux Produits et Saveurs d'Auvergne** (No. 21) for Auvergnat hams and cheeses, and **Terra Corsa** (No. 42) for Corsican specialities. As so often in Paris, upward mobility can be brilliantly observed in pâtisseries. Choose between star baker **Arnaud Delmontel** (No. 39; tel: 01 48 78 29 33) for his Renaissance baguette and cakes flavoured with yuzu, green tea or rhubarb, and the wholefood hippie ethos of franglais-owned **Rose Bakery** (No. 46; tel: 01 42 82 12 80), where you can eat in or take away carrot cake and crumble, quiches and salads. Typical of the area's mutation are eccentric bistro the **Cul de Poule** (No. 53; tel: 01 53 16 13 07) – meaning 'hen's arse' but also refering to a type of bowl used by chefs – serving good food in a junk shop decor; and the **Hôtel Amour** (8 rue de Navarin; tel: 01 48 78 31 80), gone from seedy hotel to hip, anti-design hangout. The flashing pink neon sign preserves a requisite touch of sleaze, but inside it has artist-created bedrooms and a friendly restaurant in a lovely overgrown courtyard garden.

*Sopi: map E3*

# Discover a **Parisian village** and a **modern eco park** at **Batignolles**

It's intriguing to think that if Monet hadn't exhibited *Impression, Soleil Levant* at the Salon des Refusés in 1874, the Impressionists might have been called the Batignolles School – a reflection of the period when Manet was immortalised in his studio, with Renoir, Bazille, Monet and other friends, in Fantin-Latour's *L'Atelier à Batignolles*. Like neighbouring Montmartre, Batignolles was one of the villages absorbed by Paris in 1860; but it has kept its more workaday social and racial mix and villagey authenticity, a provincial enclave between the din of boulevard des Batignolles, avenue de Clichy and the rue de Rome railway cutting.

*Paris populaire*, arty Paris and gentrified Paris converge on busy rue des Dames at **Bistro des Dames** (No. 18; tel: 01 45 22 13 42; www.eldoradohotel.fr), where you can eat in the lush garden of bohemian Hôtel Eldorado, and **Les Caves Populaires** (No. 22; tel: 01 53 04 08 32), which draws a crowd of habituées for inexpensive wines and simple dishes. Another local hub is the square in front of the pretty neoclassical church Ste-Marie de Batignolles, where **L'Endroit** (place du Dr Félix Lobligeois; tel: 01 42 29 50 00) is a cool drinking haunt by night and a favourite with families for weekend brunch – before or after a visit to **Square des Batignolles**, with its bandstand, duckpond and giant plane trees. Across rue Cardinet, the **Parc Clichy-Batignolles** couldn't be more different, a happy aftermath of Paris's botched attempt to score the 2012 Olympics. The area of railway sidings that would have become the Olympic village is instead a new park with an imaginative playground, a challenging skateboard ramp, and an ecological bent: solar panels on a converted forge, a long ditch to collect rainwater, and a pond planted with reeds and irises to clean Seine water for irrigation.

*Batignolles: map A5–C4*

# Follow trendsters to **Chez Jeannette** and the **bars of Faubourg St-Denis**

Faubourg-St-Denis was once part of a seedy Gare du Nord hinterland. Today, it's at the heart of a fast-evolving bar culture with an underground vibe, where new bars and bistros are thriving amid the Indian restaurants, Arab grocers, halal butchers, Chinese hole-in-the-wall takeaways, African hairdressers and a courtyard mosque. **Chez Jeannette** (47 rue du Fbg-St-Denis; tel: 01 47 70 30 89; www.chezjeannette. com) has become the unofficial HQ of advertising and design agency types, musicians and fashion creatives, who gather in an untouched decor of period mouldings, cheerfully ugly copper bar, ghastly wallpaper and kitsch 1940s chandeliers. Up the street, **Le Napoléon** (No. 73; tel: 01 47 70 21 36) has been revamped with a few nods at Napoleon, a fine cheeseburger and a terrace that fills up as soon as the weather perks up. **Le Martel** (3 rue Martel; tel: 01 47 70 67 56) is now a trendy eatery with trad bistro decor, and French and North African dishes.

Some of these spots keep going all day long, others are very much night-time haunts. The stunning belle époque dining room at **La Fidélité** (12 rue de la Fidelité; tel: 01 47 70 19 34; www.lafidelite.com)

is fashionable with Parisian night birds; quirky bistro **Playtime** (5 rue des Petits-Hôtels; tel: 01 44 79 03 98) is named after Jacques Tati's futuristic film, although its mood is more 50s nostalgia, with Eames chairs, metal lamps and affordable, revisited bistro cooking, and **Le Pompon** (39 rue des Petites-Ecuries; tel: 01 53 34 60 85) is a former synogogue, where lovely period panelling, a crystal chandelier and mosaic floor are now the backdrop for a pub-style bar, with a cellar space for bands and DJs.

*Faubourg-St-Denis; map G2–H1*

# Visit a *merveilleuse* in her bathroom at the **Petit Hôtel Bourrienne**

As is often in Paris, the lovely rue d'Hauteville conceals a treasure: the **Petit Hôtel Bourrienne**, a rare time capsule of the Directoire style of the 1790s – when, in the aftermath of the Revolution, little was built. It belonged first to 19th-century It girl, Fortunée Hamelin, then to Louis-Antoine Fauvelet de Bourrienne, private secretary of Napoléon, and in the 1880s to Charles Tuleu, Balzac's printer, who built the printworks at the end of the garden; his descendants still live in the house today.

Like her friend the Empress Josephine, who hailed from Martinique, Mme Hamelin came from one of the wealthy Caribbean planter families of Santa Dominica. She was one of *les Merveilleuses*, stylish women who introduced the fashion for the low-cut and free-flowing Empire dress (sign of the new frivolity amid the capital's

gilded youth after the drama of the Terror), and was notorious for promenading topless – or rather, in transparent muslin – down the Champs-Elysées. The most romantic room of the house? Surely the bathroom, with its marble floor and delicately painted ceiling, where Hamelin would entertain from her bath. But her bedroom is also a gem, decorated with tropical birds and butterflies in memory of the Caribbean.

Bourrienne brought the antechamber, dining room and salon into the Empire style of the time, with classical mouldings, striking ochre and green colour schemes and more, still intact and still very much in use today.

*Petit Hôtel Bourrienne; 58 rue d'Hauteville; tel: 01 47 70 51 14; Apr–June Sat–Sun 3–5pm, Sept–Mar Sun 3–5pm; charge; map G2*

Bastille, Belleville & Ménilmontant

Bastille, Belleville
and Ménilmontant

0   100   200   300   400   500 m
0   100   200   300   400   500 yds

# Discover victims of the Terror and an American hero at the **Cimetière de Picpus**

On a side street not far from Nation, a small cemetery contains the mass grave of thousands of victims of the Terror. While the royals were guillotined on place de la Concorde, by 1794 the guillotine had been set up on the other side of town at place du Trône Renversé (Square of the Overturned Throne) – the new name given to place du Trône before it became the more unifying **place de la Nation** it is today. Here, in just six weeks, 1,306 people were guillotined during the Terror, a last gasp of the Revolution before the fall of Robespierre.

The city of Paris requisitioned the grounds of a former convent nearby and dug two massive communal pits in which to pile the bodies brought in open carts. Later a group of noble families bought the land and created a second cemetery where they could be buried near their guillotined relatives, a select club of aristocratic names that is still a private cemetery today – although as the list of names in the chapel reveals, by far the majority of those guillotined were commoners.

Now run by nuns, the **Cimetière de Picpus** still feels isolated from the rest of the world behind high walls and a long garden. The sites of the two communal graves are marked out, and you can see the walled-up doorway where the carts entered under cover of darkness.

As for the little graveyard of aristocratic French families, its most famous incumbent is more associated with the American Revolution than the French one: Marquis La Fayette aka Général La Fayette, who fought in the American War of Independence against the British and drummed up French support. His tomb is draped in the stars and stripes.

*Cimetière de Picpus; 35 rue de Picpus; tel: 01 43 44 18 54; Tue–Sun 2–6pm; charge; map D1*
*Place de la Nation; map D2*

# Stock up on **fresh produce, oysters and banter** at **Marché d'Aligre**

People cross town for the legendary **rue d'Aligre street market** (Tue–Sun morning), famed for its low prices, stalls laden with fresh produce and stallholders' *tchatche* (banter). The adjoining covered **Marché Beauvau** (Tue–Sat morning and afternoon, Sun morning) is a smarter affair, with a fishmonger, cheese stalls, excellent butcher, wine merchant and a good Italian deli, but it is out on the street where everything happens. Towards the end of the morning prices get even lower as stalls sell off entire crates, and the range of fruit and veg – from tomatoes, artichokes and cherries from France to more exotic produce – gives a touch of rural France meets North African souk. Particularly busy on Sunday mornings when it can be almost impossible to push your way through the crowds, quieter during the week, this is a place to observe a cross-section of Parisians and absorb the repartee.

On the square, a small flea market, the only one in the city centre, is cheerfully junky, with cheap clothes around the edges and a motley mix of old china, secondhand books, jewellery and cutlery in the middle, not to mention a seemingly inexhaustible supply of ghastly vases, although

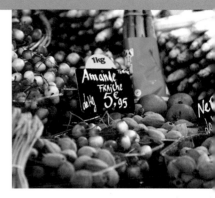

there are always a few hopefuls looking for a find.

At weekends, the convivial wine bar, **Le Baron Rouge** (1 rue Théophile Roussel; tel: 01 43 43 14 32), virtually becomes an annex of the market. Wines from all over France are chalked up on blackboards behind the bar, and you can have containers filled from barrels at the front or snack on platters of cheese and charcuterie. In winter an oyster stall sets up on the street on Sunday morning. The smart set breakfast or lunch at pretty belle époque bistro **Square Trousseau** (1 rue Antoine Vollon; tel: 01 43 43 06 00) or pick up *viennoiseries* at fashionable patisserie **Blé Sucré** (7 rue Antoine Vollon; tel: 01 43 40 77 73).

*Marché d'Aligre; map B2*

Go for a **Sunday stroll** along the **Canal St-Martin**, backdrop to chugging barges and the Hôtel du Nord

Tree-lined quays, picturesque locks, a turning bridge and green metal footbridges make the atmospheric Canal St-Martin (map A6-B8) a delightful place to amble. Between some unfortunate modern housing developments, other facades still look as if they could come from a Doisneau photo or Marcel Carné's 1938 film *Hôtel du Nord*, the old hotel now resuscitated as a fashionable bistro. At night there's a grown-up bar scene, as arty locals crowd the laidback **Chez Prune** (36 rue de Beaurepaire; tel: 01 42 41 30 47) at apéritif time or try to get a table at nearby wine bar-bistro **Le Verre Volé** (67 rue de Lancry; tel: 01 48 03 17 34). It's on Sundays, however, that the canal comes into its own, when the quays are closed to cars, the shops are open, and cyclists, families and dog-walkers turn out for a stroll or to watch the boat traffic chugging through the locks.

The canal was begun by Napoleon in 1802 and completed in 1825 to provide a short cut between the meanders of the Seine and improve the supply of drinking water to the ciy. It's still used by a surprising amount of boat traffic today, with barges carrying gravel and scrap iron, pleasure boats and boat trips on the canal run by **Canauxrama** (www.canauxrama.com) and **Paris Canal** (www.pariscanal.com).

An eclectic crowd piles into the **Hôtel du Nord** (102 quai de Jemmapes; tel: 01 40 40 78 78; www.hoteldunord.org), recently refurbished to look the perfect filmset bistro (the film was actually shot in a studio), with white metro tile walls, Art Deco bar, film lighting and assorted framed photo portraits on the walls. All slightly too good to be true but an animated, cheerful setting for a meal – better when it sticks to tradition than when it adds exotic frills.

A few doors down, behind a graffitied concrete wall, **Le Comptoir Général** (80 quai de Jemmapes; tel: 01 44 88 24 46; www.lecomptoirgeneral.com) has a more alternative mood, a cross between militant ecological group, junk shop and artist's installation, with an overgrown garden and a bric-a-brac interior. It's used for events during the week and there's an all-day bar at weekends.

On the bend of the canal, check out the fashions at **Sandro** (93 quai de Valmy); and the colourful clothes and bright global gifts and housewares inside the green, pink and yellow shopfronts of **Antoine et Lili** (No. 95). Just before Stalingrad lock, **Point Ephémère** (No. 200; tel: 01 40 34 02 48; www.pointephemere.org) is lucky enough to have a terrace stretching along the quayside. A self-proclaimed 'centre of artistic dynamics', it shares the former Point P construction materials' warehouse with a fire station and local organisations; rehearsal studios for music and dance, four artists' studios, a concert hall, exhibition space and a café-restaurant are all to be found here.

On its southern section,

between Faubourg-du-Temple and the Bastille, the canal runs under boulevard Richard-Lenoir through a long tunnel, re-emerging just south of place de la Bastille in the Port de l'Arsenal boat marina where it joins the Seine. At the northern end, on place de la Bataille de Stalingrad, is **La Rotonde de la Villette**, the grandest of all Ledoux's 18th-century neoclassical tollhouses (currently being turned into a restaurant). You can continue your walk along the broad Bassin de la Villette – one of the sites for the annual Paris Plage beach – to the Parc de la Villette (*p.156*).

# Wind down in **Parc des Buttes-Chaumont**, a park with a fantastical bent, and the **Quartier Mouzaïa**

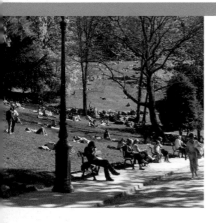

With the rolling lawns, romantic lake and mature trees of an 'English-style' garden, the picturesque **Parc des Buttes-Chaumont** was one of the new parks laid out by Napoléon III in the 1860s in his mission to bring fresh air to the people. In fact, the park is an amusing mixture of natural and fake, created over the site of old gypsum quarries that proved just perfect for conjuring up a dramatic landscape – including a lake, a craggy island crowned by a classical temple, a dramatic ravine complete with suspension bridge and a cave with fake stalactites.

You'll find all the facilities of a good local park too: puppet shows, pony rides and playgrounds for kids, plenty of lawns for lounging on, and two belle époque pavilions containing restaurant **Le Pavillon du Lac** and convivial 'restaurant-guinguette' (an open-air dance hall) **Rosa Bonheur**.

Take a look at the rest of the district too. The Haussmannian apartments overlooking the park have become highly desirable (residents include Johnny Depp and Vanessa Paradis), while across rue de Crimée, the **Quartier Mouzaïa** exudes a charm that is endearingly provincial. The triangle of tightly packed leafy streets – such as Villa Amalia, Villa de Lorraine, Villa Bellevue and Villa Claude Monet – which run off rue Hidalgo, rue du General Brunet and rue Mouzaïa, was built in 1901 like a little garden suburb to provide affordable housing for local workers. The houses couldn't be more than two storeys high because they were built over old gypsum quarries, in contrast to the 1960s tower blocks of place des Fêtes. The triangle is now a sought-after oasis of little brick houses and front gardens overflowing with wisteria and roses.

*Parc des Buttes-Chaumont; entrances rue Bozaris, rue Manin; www.paris. fr; May–Aug daily 7am–10pm, Sept 7am–9pm, Oct–Apr 7am–8pm; free; map C8*

# Relish a **timeless bistro experience** in the vicinity of the **Bastille**

Ask most Parisians where they really like going out to eat, and it's not the grand occasion temples but their favourite Paris bistro, offering good food and good value in a casual, friendly atmosphere.

**Astier** has stayed in the 1950s of painted pine skirtings and red and white napkins, but has also seamlessly changed hands from Monsieur and Madame Astier to a young team. You'll find modern seasonal dishes alongside eternal favourites, like the pickled herrings you help yourself to from a terracotta dish and a very tipsy rum baba. The wine list is renowned and the diners eclectic.

East of the Bastille, rue Paul Bert has become a foodie enclave led by the **Bistrot Paul Bert**, a convivial if slightly cliquey rendez vous for the area's young *bourgeois bohèmes*. Food is French trad, well done and

the gigantic *côte de boeuf* served for two with chunky 'peasant' chips is a treat. The same team also runs next door fish restaurant **L'Ecailleur du Bistrot**.

The cheerful all-day **Bistrot du Peintre** (*pictured*) has a gorgeous listed Art Nouveau decor of sinuous woodwork and tiled figures representing spring and summer. It's busy lunch and dinner for its Auvergnat and southwestern specialities, peppered daily with cosmopolitan suggestions such as courgette tatin with tomato sorbet.

*Astier, 44 rue Jean-Pierre-Timbaud; tel: 01 43 57 16 35; www.restaurant-astier. com; L and D daily; map B5*
*Bistrot Paul Bert, 18 rue Paul-Bert; tel: 01 43 72 24 01; L and D Tue–Sat; map C2*
*Bistrot du Peintre, 116 avenue Ledru-Rollin; tel: 01 47 00 34 39; www.bistrot dupeintre.com; L and D daily; map B2*

# Go arty in the heights of Belleville

Like many of the poorer fringes of the city, Belleville has been endlessly settled by waves of immigrants: Parisians displaced by the demolition of the slums, peasants fresh from the land, later Arabs, Africans and Chinese, Jews and Muslims, more recently, artists and designers – and all of them seem to cram into **Aux Folies** (*pictured*; 8 rue de Belleville), a frantic bar with a crazy maze of neon on the ceiling.

This is the *Paris populaire* where singer Edith Piaf was born, literally in the street outside No. 72, and where the old tenements and steep stairways familiar from the classic children's film *The Red Balloon* now mix with Chinese restaurants and modern housing projects. Beneath the **Parc de Belleville**, which descends in terraces between rue Piat and rue Jouye-Rouve, **La Forge** (25 rue Ramponneau), an old key factory, began as an artists' squat in 1991 and is now home to around 20 artists who rent studios from the municipality. Other studios can be visited in the **Belleville open studios** (www.ateliers-artistes-belleville.org) each May.

Recently a cluster of interesting art galleries have set up here too, like **Galerie Jocelyn Wolff** (78 rue Julien-Lacroix; tel: 01 42 03 05 65); **Galerie Crèvecoeur** (4 rue Jouye-Rouve; tel: 09 54 57 31 26) and **Galerie Marcelle Alix** (tel: 09 50 04 16 80), which squeeze installations and performances into twin shopfront spaces opposite cult bistro **Le Baratin** (No. 3; tel: 01 43 49 39 70), a shabby-chic favourite of superchefs and gourmets; while **Bugada & Cargnel** (7-9 rue de l'Equerre; tel: 01 42 71 72 73) hold shows in a 1930s Citroen garage.

A touch of the area's old militancy remains in the cool, edgy programming at **La Bellevilloise** (19 rue Boyer; tel: 01 46 36 07 07), a pioneering cooperative founded in 1887 turned multi-disciplinary arts centre with restaurant.

*Parc de Belleville; map C6*

# Explore the alleyways of **Faubourg St-Antoine**, where **furniture craftsmen** alternate with media folk

Faubourg-St-Antoine, and not Bastille, used to be the name given not just to a street but to this entire district, synonymous with furniture making ever since the 15th century when furniture makers were allowed to set up workshops on land belonging to the Abbaye de St-Antoine, free of the guild restrictions for craftsmen within the city wall. In the 17th and 18th centuries, the finest cabinet makers in Europe settled along here. A distinctive architecture developed where, behind street facades with their lodgings, doorways give way to long workshop-lined alleys bearing mysterious names such as Passage de la Tête Brûlée (Burnt Head Passage) and Passage de l'Ours (Bear Passage) – with a carved bear over the entrance.

Today, most of the furniture showrooms along Faubourg-St-Antoine itself have been replaced by the likes of Nike, Etam and Gap. Poke through doorways on the Faubourg and neighbouring rue de la Roquette and rue de Charonne during the week (some close at weekends) however, and there are still a surprising number of cabinet makers at work behind the scenes, though many workshops have been colonised by a breed of more contemporary creatives: photographers, radio stations, etc.

Almost on the corner of place de la Bastille, **Passage du Cheval Blanc** leads through a series of cobbled courtyards before emerging through Cité Parchappe. **Passage du Chantier** still has furniture outlets with old shopfronts and salesmen who try to lure you in off the street. **Passage de la Main d'Or** contains a Corsican restaurant and a fringe theatre, while **Passage l'Homme** (between rue de Charonne and avenue Ledru-Rollin) is a creeper-clad dream of cottages, wooden shopfronts and painted shutters.

*Faubourg St-Antoine; map A3–E1*

# Seek out Honoré, Théodore, Edith and a **raft of French stars** at **Père Lachaise cemetery**

There's an undeniable kudos to being buried at Père Lachaise, with its winding cobbled lanes lined with family sepuchres in the form of Greek temples and Byzantine churches, obelisks, Gothic chapels and Egyptian pyramids, like houses in a city of the dead.

One of four cemeteries created after the old overcrowded city churchyards had been transferred to the Catacombes (*p145*), the cemetery opened in 1804 on land that had belonged to the Jesuits and named after Louis XIV's confessor Père Lachaise. Initially, Parisians considered it too far out of town and were reluctant to be buried here, so in 1817 playwright Molière, fabulist La Fontaine and the fanciful supposed tomb of medieval lovers Abelard and Héloise were moved here to make it fashionable – bringing with them a desirability that has never waned. Concessions are now hard to come by but the cemetery remains a preferred resting place for French artists, actors and intellectuals, which have recently included singer Mano Solo and mime artist Marcel Marceau.

Père Lachaise offers a snapshot of French intellectual and political history, with countless writers, artists, actresses, scientists, generals and politicians buried here (among them Delacroix, Pissarro, Ingres, Colette, Rossini, Bizet, Proust and actress Sarah Bernhardt). Almost all of Napoleon's generals are here. Egyptologist Champollion is appropriately commemorated by an obelisk, painter Théodore Géricault has reliefs of some of his most famous works, including the *Raft of the Medusa*, Honoré de Balzac is buried with his beloved Comtesse Hanska under a bronze bust of himself, and Allan Kardec, founder of spiritism, is remembered by what looks like a prehistoric dolmen.

Some people take a very studious approach to visiting the cemetery, devotedly poring over maps to track down the famous names; but it is equally rewarding to let yourself wander at random to make your own discoveries among the forgotten poets, inventors, administrators, singers and radicals who helped shape Paris in the 19th century, or to simply admire this incredible outdoor gallery of funerary art. Sculptures include generals on horses, seafarers and their ships, mourning nymphs, stern portraits, weeping draped figures and the side-by-side bronze effigies of Croce-Spinelli and Sivel, who died in a ballooning accident at 8,600 metres on 15 April 1875. Soaring over everything, like a Greek temple on stilts, is the tallest monument in the cemetery, the 35 metre (115ft)-high monument to a certain Princesse Elisabeth de Davidoff.

The northern sector of the cemetery is less romantic with its geometrical layout but it does contain some cult tombs that draw devoted pilgrims, including that of Jim Morrison, Edith Piaf buried under a simple polished marble slab next to her last husband Theophanis Lamboukas, and Oscar Wilde, with a Cubist nude sculpted by Jacob Epstein, smothered in lipstick kisses.

Dotted around the cemetery are memorials to the Paris Commune, to municipal workers, to the Spanish Civil War and World War II deportees. Radical working-class Ménilmontant was one of the last pockets of resistance during the Paris Commune of 1871 which, in *la Semaine sanglante* (Bloody Week), culminated in a last stand in the cemetery: 147 Communards were shot by Versaillais troops in the north-east corner against the wall now known as the Mur des Fédérés and buried in a common grave, a symbol of workers' struggle for liberation.

*Cimetière Père Lachaise; boulevard du Ménilmontant; tel: 01 55 25 82 10; www.paris. fr; Mon–Fri 8am–6pm, Sat 8.30am– 6pm, Sun 9am–6pm, winter until 5.30pm; free; map D4*

E

Panthéon **D3**
Parc de Bercy **G5**
Passerelle Simone de Beauvoir **G5**
Petit Bain, Le **G4**
Piscine Josephine Baker **F5**
Perimeter Editions **C4**
Reflet Médicis, Le **C4**
Relais Christine **C4**
Requin Chagrin **D2/3**
Rouquet, Le **A5**
Salon du Panthéon **C3**
Seven Hotel **D1**
Studio des Ursulines **C2**
Studio Galande **D4**
Tea Caddy **D4**
Vanessa Bruno **B4**

## Latin Quarter, St-Germain & Seine

0   100   200   300   400   500 m

0   100   200   300   400   500 yds

N

# Spot **ostriches and dinosaurs** at the **Jardin des Plantes**

You could easily spend a whole family day out in the **Jardin des Plantes**, home to botanical garden, natural history museum and zoo, plus all the playgrounds and ice cream stalls of a local park. The place is also home to an active scientific research institute with an illustrious past: botanist Sébastien Vaillant proved the principle of pollination and plant sexuality here in 1718 with a pistachio tree still in the garden, while physics professor Henri Becquerel demonstrated radiation from uranium in the laboratory in 1896, a heritage reflected in the nearby streets which are almost all named after eminent scientists (Buffon, Cuvier, Linné, Daubenton, etc).

The gardens originated as the royal medicinal garden and botanical school of Louis XIII, open to the public since 1640. At first sight they resemble a typical formal garden with planted quadrangles and avenues of trees creating a perspective up to the natural history museum. But they also constitute an incredible botanical reserve of more than 6,000 plant species and numerous historic trees.

Particularly intereresting is the **Alpine garden** with rockeries and peat bogs of mountain species.

The **botanical school gardens** present temperate zones from around the globe, the **roseraie** has 390 varieties of roses modern and old, and a historic **labyrinth** spirals up a hill to a picturesque wrought-iron gazebo. Even the model of the stegosaurus by the rue Buffon entrance has been surrounded by the appropriate 'archaic' plants, such as ferns and horsetails.

The **ecological garden** was created in 1932, well before ecology was newsworthy, to preserve the different natural habitats of the Ile de France. A wilderness of a bird and bee garden is home to a log cabin bee house, while the imposing 19th-century **greenhouses** have recently reopened following restoration and showcase tropical ecosystems.

Scattered around the park are the assorted departments of the Muséum National d'Histoire Naturelle. Most spectacular is the **Grande Galerie de l'Evolution**, sitting like a palace at the end of the central gardens, and brilliantly renovated to display stuffed animals by habitat in the central nave. Marine animals and Arctic species occupy the ground floor, a procession of giraffes, zebras and antelopes steps out across the savannah on the first floor, and birds hang suspended as you rise up between them in glass lifts. The star curiosity is Louis XV's Indian rhinoceros, an early masterpiece of taxidermy, though slightly bulky as an old table was used for the frame.

The park also contains a mineralogy pavilion, containing a spectacular array of minerals, meteorites and crystals (closed for renovation), and paleontology and anatomy pavilions.

**La Ménagerie** is a small zoo founded in 1794 when the former royal menagerie was transferred here from Versailles. Winding paths bring you to a flamingo pool, 19th-century aviary, art deco monkey house, the ostrich paddock, wooden climbing frames where red pandas lounge and the reptarium, home to scary snakes and spiders. During the siege of Paris; hungry Parisians were forced to eat the zoo's inhabitants and it became fashionable to say you had just tasted lion.

Take a break at the snack and ice cream stand near the entrance to the Ménagerie or go for a full-scale lunch at **La Baleine** (tel: 01 40 79 80 72), with an interior inspired by the whale skeleton from the anatomy gallery, and plenty of outdoor tables.

*Jardins des Plantes; Place Valhubert (other entrances 57 rue Cuvier, 2 rue Bouffon, 36 rue Geoffroy-St-Hilaire); tel: 01 40 79 56 01; www.mnhn.fr; park daily summer 7.30am–7.45pm, winter 8am–5.30pm, Alpine garden hours vary, zoo daily 9am–6pm, museums and greenhouses Wed–Mon 10am–6pm; charge for zoo, greenhouses and museums; map F2*

# Decipher a **medieval allegory** at Cluny

The *Lady and the Unicorn* tapestry cycle is one of the great masterpieces of medieval art, an endlessly fascinating allegory of love and the senses which abounds in charm with its gentle-looking lion and smiling unicorn against the millefiore background sprinkled with rabbits and flowers. Five tapestries represent the senses: in one the lady eats from a bowl of sweetmeats (taste), in another she holds up a mirror to the unicorn who gazes at his reflection (sight), she plays a small organ (sound), holds a penant and the unicorn's horn (touch) and makes a wreath of flowers (smell). In the mysterious sixth, she stands before a tent, with the words *à mon seul désir* (to my only desire) woven into it. Opinions vary as to whether the lady is placing her necklace in the casket held by her maid or removing it, and whether it signifies love and desire or, rather, the renunciation of worldly senses.

You could easily sit for hours in the circular room where the tapestries are displayed absorbing the detail, but there are plenty of other good reasons to visit the **Musée National du Moyen-Age** (often known as Cluny). The 15th-century Gothic townhouse of the powerful abbots of Cluny makes a perfect setting for medieval works of art, with an intimate human scale that suits the intricately worked pieces. Moreover, the building combines with by far the most substantial Roman remains in Paris – the 1st-century Thermes de Cluny baths complex. The heads of the kings of Judah from Notre-Dame, knocked off during the Revolution and rediscovered in the 1970s, can be admired against a backdrop of soaring Roman masonry.

*Musée National du Moyen-Age; 5 place Paul-Painlevé; tel: 01 53 73 78 16; www.musee-moyenage.fr; Wed–Mon 9am–5.45pm; charge; map C4*

# Marvel at the unfurling **palm tree column** inside **Eglise St-Séverin**

The leering gargoyles may look suitably Gothic but inside **Eglise St-Séverin** (rue des Prêtres-St-Séverin), the overwhelming impression is one of space and light. The church, dating from the 13th to 15th centuries, has five naves and a forest of slender columns allowing you to see right through to the double ambulatory with its famous twisted 'palm tree' column from which all the ribs flow into a complex web of vaulting overhead. Artist Robert Delaunay was so fascinated by the column that he painted it frequently from 1909 to 1912. As you leave, take a look at the adjacent charnel house.

St-Séverin is at the heart of the Paris district that has most kept its medieval character, even if now filled with cheap Greek restaurants, jazz cellars and souvenir shops rather than the medieval scholars of yore. The buildings come in a comfortably eclectic mix – a 1930s art deco hotel, fine 18th-century facades and ancient tenements with sloping walls – often built over much older cellars, such as the **Caveau de la Huchette** jazz club (5 rue de la Huchette; tel: 01 43 26 65 05), where the vaulted medieval cellars provided a hangout for Rosicrucians and Revolutionaries.

Across rue St-Jacques, ancient Roman road and pilgrimage route to Compostela, is the small **Eglise St-Julien-le-Pauvre**, built in the 12th century over a Merovingian necropolis. Long used for rowdy university assemblies, it now belongs to the Melkite Greek Catholic church; icons grace the iconostasis and walls amid medieval carved capitals.

Not quite as ancient, but a monument in its own right, is the robinia tree in the adjoining garden, Paris's oldest tree planted in 1602 and now propped up by a concrete buttress. Across the street, the **Tea Caddy** (14 rue St-Julien-le-Pauvre; tel: 01 43 54 15 56) has been serving *très* British cream teas, complete with willow pattern china, since 1928.

*Eglise St-Séverin; map D4*

# Pay homage to great men on **place du Panthéon**

example of classical architecture designed on a Greek cross plan: colonnades with crisply carved Corinthian capitals and coffered dome, where Foucault hung his pendulum in 1851 to demonstrate the rotation of the Earth. Murals by Cabanal, Bonnat, Puvis de Chavannes and others illustrate episodes from Saint Geneviève's life; but the white marble sculpture *La Convention Nationale*, at the back, is defiantly republican, depicting the figure of Marianne brandishing a sword, surrounded by groups of soldiers. From April to October, you can climb up to the dome for a 360° view over the city.

France's great men (and one woman, Marie Curie) rest in the labyrinthine barrel-vaulted crypt. It's the place to pay homage to some great writers, philosophers, scientists and forgotten statesmen and an intriguing insight into the nation's self-image: the wooden tomb of Rousseau and that of Voltaire, Victor Hugo, Emile Zola and Alexandre Dumas (moved here by Jacques Chirac), not to mention Léon Gambetta's heart.

Crowning the Montagne-Sainte-Geneviève, the **Panthéon** forms one of the grand set pieces of Parisian architecture – its vast dome a landmark that can be spotted from all over the city, and its pedimented front forming a grand perspective from the Jardin du Luxembourg. Begun in 1764, the building, designed by Soufflot, was originally commissioned as a shrine for the relics of Saint Geneviève *(p.128)*, but the Revolution intervened and it was converted into a shrine to France's great men instead.

The vast interior is a very pure

*Panthéon; place du Panthéon; tel: 01 44 32 18 00; www.pantheon.monuments-nationaux.fr; daily 10am–6.30pm, winter until 6pm; charge; map D3*

# Buy from producers at **Marché Monge or Maubert** and then picnic in a **Roman arena**

Eavesdrop on a few conversations and you soon realise just how much Parisians talk about food, with the local market essential both for stocking up and as a social rendez vous at weekends. It's typical that although the Latin Quarter has three markets within a ten-minute walk of each other, each has its own afficionados. **Place Monge** (Wed, Fri, Sun 7am–2.30pm) is a great reminder that there are still market gardeners in the Ile de France and neighbouring Picardy, with producers of apples and pears, organic veg, honey and honey cakes, plus a stall of mountain hams and cheeses, fish direct from Boulogne, usually a wine producer or two, and hot roast chicken, *choucroute garnie* and Lebanese snacks if you want an instant picnic. **Place Maubert** (Tue, Thur, Sat 7am–2.30pm) has been a market for centuries – at one point

even a *marché aux mégots*, where tramps resold tobacco gleaned from fag ends. Now it's rather upmarket and pricier than Monge, with organic produce, foie gras and olive oil stalls, and excellent cheese shop Laurent Dubois at the back of the square. It's mainly food on Saturdays, while fashion and tribal art tip the balance during the week. Not officially a market but a food-shopping street, picturesque **Rue Mouffetard** (Tue–Sat morning and afternoon, Sun morning, *p.50*) has a more touristy feel, especially on Sunday when often accompanied by street musicians. But it has good cheese and other shops.

Picnic on your finds in the **Arènes de Lutèce** (47 rue Monge), the surprising remains of Paris's Roman arena, which once seated 17,000 for gladiatorial combats.

*Place Monge; map E2*

# Watch **tapestry weavers** at work at the **Manufacture des Gobelins**

Since the magnificent **Galerie des Gobelins** reopened in 2007, it's put on some impressive shows on themes ranging from modern design to Renaissance tapestries. The gallery is however much more than a museum: it's the frontispiece for a working tapestry factory, whose weaving workshops you can visit. Tapestries are still made painstakingly by hand on big vertical looms just as they were in the factory's previous incarnation as the Manufacture Royal des Tapisseries – founded by Colbert, Louis XIV's minister of finance, in 1662, on the site where Jehan Gobelin set up his dye workshops by the Bièvre river in the 15th century – and sometimes in the very same buildings. In fact most of the original 17th-century architecture remains, including the old laboratory where dyes were mixed. All the wools are still hand-dyed here and as many as 170 different shades employed in a single tapestry.

The factory is now a state institution. Most of the tapestries are created in collaboration with contemporary artists, generally for government ministries or embassies (places that can wait four or five years). It's impressive to see how the weavers work

from an original photograph or painting, painstakingly matching colours and translating a small image into wool, blown up to 3–4 metres/10–13ft high. Strike lucky and you may time it right to witness a *Tomber du métier* – the moment when the finished tapestry is finally cut off the loom and first hung up to view.

*Manufacture des Gobelins, 42 avenue des Gobelins; tel: 01 44 08 53 49; www. mobiliernational.culture.gouv.fr; gallery (during exhibitions) Tue–Sun 11am–6pm, visits (tel: 0892 68 46 94) Tue–Thur 1pm, plus 3pm during school holidays; charge; map E1*

# Follow **Orwell and Hemingway** to literary haunts on **the Mouff**

Ever since Rabelais caroused at the Pomme du Pin on place de la Contrescarpe, the **Mouffetard district** has drawn partying Sorbonne students and writers in search of inspiration. The area is still marked by the expats who fuelled a literary effervescence here between the wars, drawn by inexpensive restaurants and cheap lodgings. Today **Café Delmas** and **Café La Contrescarpe** compete with their pavement terraces, **Le Requin Chagrin** attracts a studenty set, and a painted sign of Au Nègre Joyeux is still visible over a small supermarket. George Orwell lived in a seedy hotel in rue du Pot-de-Fer in 1928-9 while he worked as *plongeur* (washer up) at the Hôtel Lotti, gathering material for *Down and Out in Paris and London*, – in which the street is called rue du Coq d'Or: 'a ravine of tall, leprous houses, lurching towards one another in queer attitudes, as though they had all been frozen in the act of collapse. All the houses were hotels and packed to the tiles with lodgers, mostly Poles, Arabs and Italians. At the foot of the hotels were tiny BISTROs, where you could be drunk for the equivalent of a shilling.' The hotels have gone but the street is still filled with inexpensive restaurants.

In 1921, James Joyce completed *Ulysses* while staying in an apartment at 71 rue du Cardinal-Lemoine, lent to him by his translator, Valéry Larbaud (only the rural-looking lane leading to the courtyard is visible from the street). The book, which had been banned for obscenity in Britain and the USA, was published first in Paris – in rue de l'Odéon – in a tiny edition by Sylvia Beach in February 1922. Also in 1922, a young Ernest Hemingway and his wife Hadley lodged in a flat at 74 rue du Cardinal-Lemoine, later moving round the corner to 39 rue Descartes, the building where poet Paul Verlaine died in 1896. It is now a restaurant called **La Maison de Verlaine**.

*Rue Mouffetard; map D2*

# Discuss with film directors at Paris's **oldest picture house** – the **Cinéma du Panthéon**

Paris's oldest surviving cinema, the **Cinéma du Panthéon** (13 rue Victor-Cousin; www. whynotproductions.fr; map C3), opened in 1907, just 12 years after the Lumière brothers organised the world's very first public film screening at the Jockey Club (now Hôtel Scribe). The cinema marked its centenary with the creation of the **Salon du Panthéon** (tel: 01 56 24 88 80; Mon–Fri noon–7pm; map C3) above the auditorium, decorated by Catherine Deneuve with squashy sofas, pouffes and flea market finds and now a cult insider address for its quiches, salads, and tempting cakes.

Screening an incredible selection of films every week, and with more than 800 film shoots occurring in the city every year, Paris is a wonderful destination for film buffs. The Latin Quarter is the heart of cinephile Paris, with its dedicated bunch of small arts cinemas. As well as the Cinéma du Panthéon, there are **Le Grand Action** (5 rue des Ecoles; www. actioncinemas.com) and its sibling **Le Desperado** (No. 23), which specialise in Hollywood classics; **Studio des Ursulines** (10 rue des Ursulines; www.studiodesursulines. com), with vintage decor and a programme of children's films; the rue Champollion trio, **Le Reflet Médicis** (No.3; www.lesecransde paris.com), **La Filmothèque du Quartier Latin** (No. 9; www. lafilmotheque.fr) and **Le Champo** (51 rue des Ecoles; www.lechampo. com); eclectic **Espace Saint Michel** (7 place St-Michel; http:// cinemasaintmichel.free.fr), where Iranian films are as likely as Woody Allen; or 83-seat **Studio Galande** (42 rue Galande; www. studiogalande.fr) – the *Rocky Horror Picture Show* is a fixture every Friday and Saturday night.

*Cinemas and Studios; map C2-4, D3-4, E3*

# Join St-Germain **café society**

When it comes to boulevard St-Germain there's only one question to be asked: are you Flore or are you Magots? Paris's two most famous cafés, **Café de Flore** (*pictured*; 172 boulevard St-Germain; tel: 01 45 48 55 26) and **Les Deux Magots** (6 place St-Germain-des-Prés; tel: 01 45 48 55 25) still draw the (g)literati – now mingled with the international jet set and tourists. The legendary duo form an intriguingly self-perpetuating literary tradition, still favoured by writers for interviews and rendezvous, each one awarding its own literary prize. It boils down to a question of taste: the Deux Magots with its painted wooden statues of the two *magots* or magi (wise men), its regulars for weekend breakfast, and shielded terrace; or, the Flore, with its red banquettes and art deco lights, and service with a dry sense of humour delivered by imperturbable waiters in waistcoats and white aprons. The Flore drew the Surrealists in the 1920s, Sartre and De Beauvoir during the

war when they came here to write by the warm stove, singers Juliette Gréco and Serge Gainsbourg, now succeeded by a new generation. Today's *germanopratines* (St-Germain's female residents) favour the interior, lunch regulars prize the first floor.

Meanwhile, politicians go for stuffier **Brasserie Lipp** (151 boulevard St-Germain) across the street. **Le Rouquet** (No. 188; map A5) is a temple to 1950s neon and formica, while young trendies kiss cheeks on the terrace at **Le Bar du Marché** (75 rue de Seine), with its corner vantage point over the rue du Buci food shops.

*Boulevard and Place St-Germain; map B4*

# Pick up the best of **modern design** in the **St-Germain gallery district**

Rue de Seine, at the heart of the St-Germain gallery district, has become a treasure trove for sought-after modern design classics, designed in the 1940s and 50s by avant-garde architects. At **Galerie Downtown** (tel: 01 46 33 82 41), François Laffanour has two galleries, showing contemporary designers like Ron Arad, Gaetano Pesce and the sculptural balancing acts of Korean Byung Hoon Choi at No. 33; and 1950s design classics, such as Serge Mouille's spider-like 1950s black metal lamps and the output of Jean Prouvé, across the street.

**Galerie Matthieu Richard** (*pictured*; No. 34; tel: 01 56 24 44 87) specialises in the pierced metal furniture by Mathieu Matégot. **Jousse Entreprise** (No. 18; tel: 01 53 82 13 60) is an expert on Jean Prouvé, and here you might find sections of Prouvé's innovative prefabricated buildings as well as his furniture, along with designers such as Charlotte Perriand, Pierre Paulin and ceramicist Georges Jouve. At **Galerie Jacques Lacoste** (No. 12; tel: 01 40 20 41 82), the predeliction is for Jean Royère, a fashionable decorator of the 1940s.

Another gallery that works with contemporary designers is **Perimeter Editions** (47 rue St-André des Arts; tel: 01 55 42 01 22), set in a beautiful *hôtel particulier* where it produces limited editions with designers such as Mathieu Lehanneur and Paola Petrobelli.

For lunch, gallerists decamp to **La Palette** (No. 43; tel: 01 43 26 68 15), the archetypal Art Nouveau artist's café, with palettes hanging over the bar and pavement tables for a steak tartare or croque monsieur; or to cheerful bistro and wine bar **Fish La Boissonnerie** (No. 69; tel: 01 43 54 34 69; map B4), set behind the mosaic shopfront of a former *poissonnerie* (fishmonger).

*St Germain; map B5*

Take a pew in one of the iconic green chairs of the **Jardin du Luxembourg** to watch Parisians at play

The classic Parisian park with sculptures, a bandstand and all the activities and facilities for garden-starved apartment dwellers, the **Jardin du Luxembourg** is not so much old-fashioned as timeless: a palimpsest of Parisian life, with its pétanque pitches, tennis courts, cafés, playgrounds and sandpits, go carts, pony rides, cast-iron carousel, and a circular pond where generations of children have hired toy sailing boats in summer. One thing the Luxembourg gardens has made its own is the green metal Luxembourg chair, a desirable attribute for practising the *très* Parisian art of people-watching.

The Jardin began life as the private gardens of the Palais de Luxembourg (now the Sénat), built in 1614 in Renaissance Mannerist style inspired by the Pitti Palace in Florence for Marie de Médicis, when she no longer wanted to live in the Louvre after the assassination of Henri IV. There are gravel paths and lawns, bee hives where you can take courses in beekeeping and heritage collections of neatly espaliered apple and pear trees. The gardens are also like a mini museum of sculpture, with the white stone figures of the queens of France providing a splendid evocation of fashion down the centuries and a sort of proto-feminist recognition of obscure women. Most dramatic is the Médicis fountain modelled on Renaissance grottoes, a giant cyclops looming over the romantically gloomy carp pool.

*Jardin du Luxembourg; place Edmond-Rostand/boulevard St-Michel/rue Guynemer/rue de Vaugirard; www.senat.fr; daily, times vary between Dec–Jan 8.15am–4.45pm and June–mid July 7.30am–9.30pm; free; map B3*

Go aquatic in the **new east** with a dip in a **floating swimming pool** and nautical nightlife to follow

The four L-shaped towers of the **Bibliothèque Nationale François Mitterrand**, France's new national library, herald the Paris Seine Rive Gauche development area, dubbed the 'new Latin Quarter', growing on the place of old railway sidings and warehouses. Despite its aura of big statement architecture as the last of Mitterrand's *Grands Projets*, the library designed by Dominique Perrault is actually a building that works better on the inside than out, with a glazed corridor running all round the central well – which contains an imported pine wood – reading rooms open to all, and temporary exhibitions.

Unlike many new districts mainly devoted to business, here there's a surprisingly successful mix: a university, residential, business and even entertainment district, where new buildings are interspersed with parks and traces of the area's industrial past. During the week it buzzes with students and office workers, at weekends it's more likely to be cinema-goers heading for the 14-screen **MK2 Bibliothèque** multiplex.

From the library, spot the artfully graffitied concrete of **Les Frigos** (rue des Frigos; www.les-frigos. com), old refrigerated warehouses, home to more than 200 artists, musicians, photographers and craftspeople. Artists here were the first to colonise the district and campaigned to keep some of the industrial heritage. Rusty refrigeration pipes still run through some of the studios; visit in the annual *portes ouvertes* (open house) in May. Further along, the Moulins de Paris flour mills have had a stylish conversion into a new university library, while along the quays, the 1890s compressed air building with modern extension is now an architecture school.

Behind the library, the broad avenue de France has been laid out, a frontier between brave new world and old Paris. Spot the homage to Astérix's creator in rue René Goscinny, where speech bubbles adorn lampposts, and the Biopark, its buildings covered in a tangle of climbing plants.

On the waterfront, the Port de la Gare has become a new entertainment hub, with the **Piscine Josephine Baker** (tel: 01 56 61 96 50; www.paris.fr), a floating swimming pool with a retractable roof and sunbathing deck in summer, and a cluster of lively music bars. Red steel lighthouse ship **Batofar** (tel: 09

**ACROSS THE RIVER**

The **Passerelle Simone de Beauvoir**, Paris's 37th and newest bridge, was ingeniously designed by Austrian architect Dietmar Feichtinger to give you a choice of routes – from the deck of the Bibliothèque Nationale or down at quay level, above or below – to the **Parc de Bercy** across the river, a modern park created where wine used to be brought in on barges (although the area has also gained an ominous association with taxes since the **Ministry of Finance** moved here). The strange grass-covered pyramid is the **Palais Omnisports de Paris-Bercy** indoor stadium used for sports and rock concerts, then there's the **Cinémathèque de Paris** repertory cinema and film museum (originally designed by Frank Gehry as the American Centre) and **Cour St-Emilion**, old wine warehouses converted into wine bars, cafés and boutiques. *Map G4–5*

71 25 50 61; www.batofar.org) is one of Paris's best clubs with a bar and restaurant. **La Dame de Canton** (www.damedecanton. com) puts on eclectic live music and DJs in a Chinese sailing junk, while purple Bateau El Alamein veers more towards chanson and jazz. The latest arrival is **Le**

**Petit Bain** (www.petitbain.org), a yellow barge that offers music, performance and a restaurant.

*Bibliothèque Nationale François Mitterrand; quai François Mauriac; tel: 01 53 79 59 59; Tue–Sat 10am–7pm, Sun 1–7pm, closed 2 weeks Sept; charge; map F4*

# Find Racine, Pascal and the shrine of Paris's patron saint at **St-Etienne-du-Mont**

If the Panthéon is echoing and imposing, the beautiful church of **St-Etienne-du-Mont**, niched in a corner of the same square, is glowing and intimate. Because of the Panthéon's change of use, the shrine of Saint Geneviève, patron saint of Paris, was brought here instead when adjoining Eglise Ste-Geneviève was demolished in 1804, bringing with it a particularly Parisian appeal. With construction dragging on between 1492 and 1665, St-Etienne-du-Mont has a happy mix of Renaissance and Gothic styles all of its own. The facade has stacked classical

pediments, sculpted fruit swags and statues. Inside, Gothic vaulting combines with classical arches and balustrades and the only roodscreen to survive in Paris, a Renaissance masterpiece with ornate strapwork, double spiral staircase, and reliefs of angels. Admire the impressive wooden pulpit, held up by a sturdy Samson. In the chapel behind the choir, two plaques mark the burial spot of former parishioners Jean Racine and Blaise Pascal.

Geneviève is credited with saving the city from Attila the Hun in AD 451; her richly decorated shrine and neo-Gothic chapel is next to the choir – a pseudo-medieval bronze case contains a stone tombstone that has indeed been dated to the 5th century. A remnant of the old Eglise Ste-Geneviève can be spotted on rue Clovis, where the medieval Tour Clovis sticks up amid former monastic buildings, now prestigious Lycée Henri-IV.

*Eglise St-Etienne-du-Mont; place Ste-Geneviève; tel: 01 43 54 11 79; www.saint etiennedumont.fr; Sept–June Tue–Fri 8.45am-7.30pm, closed noon-2.30pm in school hols, Sat–Sun 8.45am–noon, 2-7.45pm; July–Aug Tue–Sun 10am–noon, 4-7.15pm; free; map D3*

# Touch down in **Zaha Hadid's pavilion** at the **Institut du Monde Arabe**

The **Institut du Monde Arabe** may be a centre for Arabic culture but it is equally a destination for anyone interested in modern architecture, all the more so since Jean Nouvel's original building was joined in 2011 by Zaha Hadid's flying-saucer-like **Mobile Art** gallery. Looking like a shiny white doughnut that has just landed on the forecourt by the institute, Anglo-Iraqi architect Zaha Hadid's sleek white structure was originally designed for Chanel as a travelling gallery, made out of lightweight panels that could be packed up in crates and shipped around the world. Reconstructed here for temporary exhibitions, its distorted torus form is a sculpture in its own right, with an interior that doesn't seem to have a vertical wall in sight.

Next door, the original institute was one of the most successful of President Mitterrand's *Grands Projets*, a brilliant modern interpretation of Arab architecture in glass and steel. Financed by 19 Arab countries, Nouvel called it 'a hinge between two cultures and two histories': one side with complex, articulated steel shutters recalling the carved wood screens of traditional Arab buildings, the other glazed to reflect the cityscape across the Seine. The Institut has a library, shop, cinema and auditorium. On the first floor, the museum explores Islamic heritage, through beautiful tiles and ceramics, embroidered fabrics, scientific instruments and Persian miniatures. Take one of the glass lifts to Lebanese restaurant Noura, with an astonishing view of Paris from the roof terrace.

*Institut du Monde Arabe, 1 rue des Fossés-Saint-Bernard; tel: 01 40 51 38 38; www. imarabe.org; Tue–Sun 10am–6pm; charge; map E3*

# Invalides and Montparnasse

0  100  200  300  400  500 m
0  100  200  300  400  500 yds

**A** **B** **C** **D** **E**

**1** **2** **3** **4** **5** **6** **7** **8**

QUAR
LATIN

Musée
Delacroix

Rue Bonaparte

ST-GERMAIN-
DES-PRÉS

St-Germain-
des-Prés

Rue du Four

Port des Saints-Pè

Port des Tuileries

Quai des Tuileries

Quai Voltaire

Le Voltaire

Brimo de
Laroussilhe

Galerie
Chevalier

Anne-Marie Monin

Rue de Verneuil

St-Thomas-
d'Aquin

Rue de Lille

MUSÉE
D'ORSAY
Musée d'Orsay

Rue de l'Université

R. du Bac

Bd. St-Germain

Editions du Parfum
Frédéric Malle

Rue de Grenelle

SÈVRES
BABYLONE

Boulevard Raspail

Hugo &
Victor

Rue du Bac

Bon
Marché

La Grande Epicerie

Rue de Babylone

Pâtisserie des Rêves

Musée Maillol

Barthélemy

RUE DU BAC

Port de Solferino

Quai Anatole France

Boulevard St-Germain

SOLFERINO

Rue de Belle-chasse

Hôtel
Matignon

Rue de Varenne

Rue de Grenelle

La Pagode

R. Vanea

Rue Barbet de Jouy

Port de la Concorde

Concorde

Elysées

Seine

ASSEMBLÉE
NATIONALE

Pl. du
Palais Bourbon

Assemblée
Nationale
(Palais Bourbon)

Rue Saint-Dominique

Basilique
Ste-Clotilde

VARENNE

Musée
Rodin

Rue de Varenne

Lycée
Victor
Duruy

ST-FRANÇOIS
XAVIER

Pl. du Prés.
Mitbourd

St-François

Cours la Reine

Cours la Reine

Port des Ch

Port de la Conférence

Port du Gros Caillou

INVALIDES

INVALIDES

Av. du Mal. Galliéni

Pl. des
Invalides

Musée
de l'Armée

Hôtel des
Invalides

St-Louis

Musée des
Plans-reliefs

Église
du Dôme

JARDIN DE
L'INTENDANT

Pl. Vauban

Boulevard des Invalides

Av. de Villars

Avenue de Breteuil

LA TOUR
MAUBOURG

Boulevard de

Av. de Tourville

Pl. de Tourville

Av. de

Ségur

Roosevelt

Pont de l'Alma

Port de Paris

Port du Gros Caillou

Egouts de Paris

American
Church in Paris

Rue de l'Université

St-Pierre-du-
Gros-Caillou

R. Malar

L'Ami Jean

Thoumieux/
Restaurant de
Jean-François Piège

La Tour Maubourg

Rue Surcouf

Rue Saint-Dominique

Rue de Grenelle

La Fontaine
de Mars

Av. Bosquet

Le Violon d'Ingres

Les Cocottes

Rue Cler

Rue de Grenelle

Rue Augereau

Hôtel du
Champs de
Mars

Av. du Champ de Mars

Av. de La Bourdonnais

Avenue de La Motte Picquet

ÉCOLE
MILITAIRE

Avenue Duquesne

R. d'Estrées

École
Militaire

Avenue de Lowendal

Pl. de

Avenue de La Motte Picquet

DUPLEIX

Port de

Port de l'Alma

Musée d'Art
Moderne de la
Ville de Paris

ALMA
MARCEAU

Pont de l'Alma

Café
Constant

Pl. du Général
Gouraud

Rue de l'Université

Rue Jean
Jacques Rueff

Av. Fr. le Play

PONT DE
L'ALMA

Musée du
Quai Branly

Quai Branly

Avenue de la Bourdonnais

Avenue Charles Floquet

CHAMP
DE
MARS

Pl.
Joffre

Allée Thomy Thierry

Avenue de Suffren

PARC
DU
CHAMP

Tour Eiffel

Av. Gustave Eiffel

St-Léon

Pl. Dupleix

Avenue de la Fédération

Avenue de Suffren

15e

7e

Port de la Bourdonnais

Avenue de New York

Quai Branly

N

L'Ami Jean **37**

Anne-Marie Monin **E6**

Barthélemy **D5**

Bon Marché **D5**

Brimo de Larcussilhe **E6**

Café Constant **B6**

Catacombes de Paris, Les **E1**

Closerie des Lilas, La **E3**

Cocottes, Les **B6**

Coupôle, La **D3**

Dôme, Le **D3**

Éditions du Parfum
Frédéric Malle **D5**

Église du Dôme **C6**

Égouts de Paris **B7**

Fondation Henri
Cartier-Bresson **D2**

Fontaine de Mars, La **B6**

Galerie Chevalier **E6**

Grande Épicerie, La **D5**

Hôtel des Invalides **C6**

Hôtel du Champs de Mars **B6**

Hugo & Victor **D5**

Montparnasse 1900 **E3**

Musée Bourdelle **D3**

Musée d'Orsay **D6**

Musée de l'Armée **C6**

Musée des Plans-reliefs **C5**

Musée du Montparnasse **D3**

Musée du Quai Branly **A7**

Musée Maillol **D5**

Musée Rodin **C6**

Musée Zadkine **E3**

Pagode, La **C5**

Pâtisserie des Rêves **D5**

Restaurant de Jean-François
Piège **B6**

Rosebud **D3**

Rotonde, La **E3**

Select, Le **D3**

Solar Hôtel **E1**

Thoumieux **B6**

Tour Eiffel **A6**

Violon d'Ingres, Le **B6**

Voltaire, Le **E6**

133

# View the **giants of Impressionism** in the setting of a converted railway station at **Musée d'Orsay**

You could hardly find a better setting for Impressionist paintings than the converted Gare d'Orsay train station, with its grandiose coffered vault and sculpture displayed where trains once pulled in. The Impressionists were artists of the steam age, inspired by the modernity of train travel (Monet's *Gare St-Lazare*), dance halls (Renoir), the ballet (Degas) and watersports, and taking the train to flit to the beach at Trouville.

The collection contains an astonishing hit list of Impressionism: five of Monet's *Rouen Cathedral* series, views of the garden at Giverny, Manet's *Déjeuner sur l'Herbe* and *L'Olympia*, Degas's racehorses, ballerina pastels and bronzes, before Post-Impressionist icons by Cézanne, Gauguin and Van Gogh. But the collection running from 1848 to 1906 is much broader than Impression – fortunately so, as the Impressionist galleries tend to be the most crowded – also taking in the decorative arts, sculpture and early photography as well as more painting. Don't miss Daumier's wonderful caricature heads, depicting different character traits in the politicians of the time. You can assess Symbolist works by Puvis de Chavannes and Moreau, and reevaluate the official *art pompier* by artists such as Cabanel and Bouguereau, who used mythological subjects as an excuse for acres of pearly flesh. A wonderful array of Nabis works ranges from Vuillard's decorative panels of public parks to Bonnard's brilliantly simplified cat.

For a final taste of train travel, have lunch amid chandeliers and painted ceilings at the splendid restaurant (tel: 01 45 49 47 03).

*Musée d'Orsay; 1 rue de la Légion d'Honneur; tel: 01 40 49 48 14; www.musee-orsay.fr; Tue–Sun 9.30am–6pm, Thur until 9.45pm; charge; map D6*

# Follow the banks of the Seine for **books, antiques and curios**

Marking the psychological and physical divide between Left Bank and Right Bank, a stroll along the River Seine provides a panorama of many of the city's greatest monuments, from the Bibliothèque de France in the east to the Eiffel Tower in the west. Plenty of stairways allow you to walk along the street-level quays or descend to the riverside banks for waterside views sprinkled with houseboats and café barges.

It's also a place of commerce and curios. Pont de Sully sees the first of the dark green boxes of the *bouquinistes*, in which the wares of second-hand book and printsellers are padlocked at night and unveiled in the afternoons in a more or less non-stop procession along the Latin Quarter and St-Germain quays (and to a lesser extent on the other side of the river, too). Some are generalists, others specialise in politics, biographies, crime novels or illustrated books, or show off old magazine covers from *L'Aurore* or *Paris Match*.

At quai Voltaire, often dubbed 'quai des Antiquaires', it's the turn of antique shops, which occupy the fine riverside residences in a showcase that includes medieval enamels and Renaissance objets d'art at **Brimo de Laroussilhe** (No.

7), tapestries and textiles at **Galerie Chevalier** (No. 17) and 18th-century furniture at **Anne-Marie Monin** (No. 27). A great time to visit is at the end of May, when the dealers of the Carré Rive Gauche (the square formed by quai Voltaire and rues de Beaune, Lille and Bac) bring out their exceptional treasures or rare discoveries.

Good places to eat along quai des Grands-Augustins include superb Spanish restaurant **Fogon** (No. 45; tel: 01 43 54 31 33) and Guy Savoy's appropriately named, chic bistro **Les Bouquinistes** (No. 53; tel: 01 43 25 45 94). Or, join the antique dealers at distinguished, if pricey, historic brasserie **Le Voltaire** (27 quai Voltaire; tel: 01 42 61 17 49).

*Quai Voltaire; map D–E6*

# Feel the might of **Napoleon**, one-time ruler of half of Europe, and see his tomb at **Les Invalides**

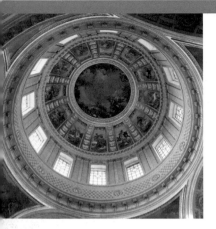

Two immense megalomaniacs come face to face at Les Invalides: the Sun King Louis XIV and the Emperor Napoleon. Louis XIV built the imposing classical complex as a grandiose retirement home for soldiers wounded in his countless wars (hence the name), bringing in his finest architects Libéral Bruand and Jules Hardouin-Mansart to design the double church, vast *cour d'honneur* with its sundials and two storeys of arcades, and facades sculpted with military trophies. An equestrian relief of the king overlooks the esplanade, while Napoleon gazes down over the *cour d'honneur*.

The Eglise du Dôme – visible from all over Paris with its shiny gilding – contains the red porphyry tomb of Napoleon, transferred here in 1840 from the island of Saint Helena where he had died. In the crypt around it, relief friezes that tell of the emperor's achievements are a fascinating piece of pompous hagiography for a figure who at one point ruled half of Europe (don't expect mentions of Waterloo or Trafalgar here) and created systems of government and education still largely in place.

Much of the rest of Les Invalides is devoted to the **Musée de l'Armée**, telling the military history of France since the Middle Ages through endless galleries of armour and beautifully engraved weapons, Napoleon's frock coat and black hat (apparently he had several), to powerful film footage of the D-Day Landings. The **Historial de Gaulle** is a multi-screen audiovisual presentation of the general's role in World War II and the liberation of France. More of an oddity is the **Musée des Plans-reliefs**: giant scale models of fortified French cities, originally used for planning military strategy.

*Les Invalides; 129 rue de Grenelle;*
*tel: 01 44 42 38 77; www.invalides.org;*
*daily, Apr–Sept 10am–6pm, Oct–Mar*
*10am–5pm, closed 1st Mon of the month;*
*charge; map C6*

# Count the figures on the Gates of Hell at the
## Musée Rodin

The Hôtel Biron, the 18th-century mansion and spacious gardens where Rodin lived towards the end of his life, provides a beautiful setting for his work and numerous insights into what made him such a revolutionary sculptor and a bridge between the 19th-century and modern art. Different versions of *St John the Baptist* or *The Walking Man* go from realist to armless, as the artist reworked the theme. They show the incredible freedom of his approach to the body as he took inspiration from antique sculpture to cut off arms or legs, also visible in blocks of marble where portraits and nudes emerge from rough unfinished stone. Upstairs there are plaster figures and composition studies for the *Burghers of Calais*, studies for the monument to Balzac on boulevard Raspail, and paintings by Van Gogh, Renoir and some of the other artists collected by Rodin.

One room is devoted to the tormented sculptures of Camille Claudel, Rodin's young pupil and mistress, including the extraordinary *The Wave* with bronze figures of bathers dwarfed by a giant green marble wave.

After visiting the house, the towering bronze *The Gates of Hell*, outside, now appears rather like a summary of Rodin's art, swarming with small versions of many of the sculptures visible in the house – including *Three Shades*, *Ugolino*, and the famous *The Thinker*.

Many more sculptures are dotted around the gardens, while temporary exhibitions are put on in the restored chapel. The museum has a popular, relaxed outdoor café, or you might also go to **La Pagode** (57 bis rue de Babylone; tel: 01 45 55 48 48), a lovely Japanese pagoda cinema which has a tea room in its tranquil Japanese garden.

*Musée Rodin; 79 rue de Varenne; tel: 01 44 18 61 10; www.musee-rodin.fr; Tue–Sun 10am–5.45pm; charge; map C6*

Get right down under the belly of the **Iron Lady** for the **most spine-tingling views**

Among nicknames for the **Eiffel Tower** are *la dame de fer* (the iron lady) and *la grande oreille* (the big ear), the latter relating to the use of its radio station to listen in on enemy messages during World War I. Intended to show off France's engineering prowess for the World Fair of 1889, on the centenary of the French Revolution, the tower was significantly constructed on the Champ de Mars, the former military parade ground where celebrations for the anniversary of the Revolution were held in the 1790s. At 300 metres/984ft (today, 324 metres/1,063ft with radio aerials) it was the tallest building in the world. As with many modern arrivals, Gustave Eiffel's structure was initially feared or detested by many. During its construction,

Garnier, Dumas fils and Maupassant were among those who signed a petition against it, poet François Coppée wrote 'the monster is hideous', 'an ugly colossus' and 'a Yankee dream', while William Morris claimed to go up it every day for lunch simply to avoid having to see it from afar. But Gustave Eiffel defended his project: 'I believe, for my part, that the tower will have its own beauty.' In the end it was completed in just two years, two months and five days, and opinions soon changed. The fascinating structure drew nearly two million visitors during the world fair and now regularly receives 7 million visitors a year.

The tower was intended to be temporary, but was saved by its role in telecommunications: France's first wireless transmission was made from here to the Panthéon in 1898, from 1903 it was used for military transmissions, and during World War I, the big ear intercepted crucial messages during the Battle of the Marne. It is still used for radio broadcasts and, since 2005, for TNT.

Naturally, most people climb to the top for the views over Paris; but the really exciting views to be had are those of the Iron Lady herself. The metal structure looks impressive as you walk underneath its four legs or as you rise up in the vintage double decker lifts, passing a constantly changing spider's web of metal girders and the 2.5 million rivets that hold them together. Two stops punctuate the way up. The first level has the **58 Eiffel brasserie** (located 58 metres above ground level), souvenir shops and an ice rink at Christmas. Gourmet restaurant **Jules Verne** (tel: 01 45 55 61 44) is on the second level at 115 metres/377ft (reached by its own lift). The third level at 275 metres/984ft brings you to Gustave Eiffel's cosy office, a champagne bar and a viewing deck. The tower sparkles nightly with thousands of tiny lights, on the hour from nightfall until 1am.

One thing has changed recently. Queuing was always part of the Eiffel Tower experience, but you can now book in advance over the web. Should you arrive ticketless, note that queues are usually shorter on foggy days or late at night.

*Eiffel Tower; Champ de Mars; tel: 08 92 70 12 39; www.tour-eiffel.fr; mid-June–Aug daily 9am–midnight, last lift to top 11pm, Sept–mid-June daily 9.30am–11pm, last lift to top 10.30pm; charge; map A6*

# Pose for sculptor Maillol on rue de Grenelle, where the **Musée Maillol** occupies a **lovely mansion**

In the early 18th century when the Marais had gone out of fashion, nobles and civil servants jostled to put up mansions just outside the city walls in the Faubourg St-Germain. Streets like rue de Grenelle, rue de Varenne and rue Vaneau are still lined with these residences, many of them now embassies and government ministries. The **Musée Maillol** is a rare one that can be visited, with Aristide Maillol's sculptures, modern art and excellent temporary exhibitions displayed around the panelled rooms of the beautiful Hôtel Bouchardon.

The museum was created in 1995 by Dina Vierny as a tribute to Maillol, but it also tells you a lot about diminutive, Romanian-born Vierny, who first posed for the elderly sculptor in 1934 when aged only 15. She was the model for some of his most celebrated sculptures, such as *Spring*, *Air* and *Harmony*, proving the perfect beauty for his idealised classical forms. She also sat for other artists including Matisse and Dufy. Later, as a collector and gallerist, she gathered drawings by Matisse and Picasso, Surrealist objects by Marcel Duchamp and championed Russian artists and naive painters. The museum covers all stages of Maillol's career, including tapestries, ceramics and little-known early paintings and pastels when he was associated with the Nabis.

The museum has a pleasant Italian café in the cellar. In the street outside is the splendid Fountain of the Four Seasons, sculpted by Edmé Bouchardon in 1739-45, with allegorical figures representing the city of Paris.

*Musée Maillol; 61 rue de Grenelle; tel: 01 42 22 59 58; www.museemaillol.com; daily 10.30am–7pm, Fri until 9.30pm; charge; map D5*

# Explore **non-Western cultures** at the **Musée du Quai Branly**

An enormous success since it opened in 2005, the **Musée du Quai Branly** is the culmination of former President Chirac's pet project to create a showcase for art from non-Western cultures; for which Jean Nouvel's long colourful building, perched on stilts in an increasingly jungle-like wild garden created by Gilles Clément, provides a baroque and other-worldly environment. Inside, a large ramp curves up to the permanent collection, which is arranged in four zones: Asia, Africa, the Americas and Oceania. Although colour-coded by continent, it is also intended to span cultures and allow you to wander from one to the other.

The displays go beyond the usual preconceptions of tribal art with an incredible variety of items, from Gabonese masks, North American Indian painted cowhides and astonishing carved beams and lintels from Papua New Guinea, to modern Aboriginal paintings – with photographs, film footage and sound recordings enhancing the experience. The emphasis is on theatricality and aura rather than a dry academic take. Many cases are dimly lit, partly for conservation reasons, partly to create a sense of magic. Some items, such as the fragile Ethiopian religious paintings, are displayed shrine-like in the 27 boxes that protrude from the building's facade.

A huge collection of musical instruments is stored in view in a large glass core that rises up through the building, fitting in with the transversal approach. As well as the exhibitions programme, concerts, theatre and dance are performed in either the auditorium or outdoor amphitheatre.

*Musée du Quai Branly; 37 quai Branly; tel: 01 56 61 70 00; www.quaibranly. fr; Tue, Wed, Sun 11am-7pm, Thur-Sat 11am-9pm; charge; map A7*

# Dream about **cake** at the **Pâtisserie des Rêves** and **Hugo & Victor**

Let them eat cake (or rather, brioche), Marie-Antoinette tactlessly remarked on the fate of the hungry populace, but who would have thought that designer cakes would became the showground for 21st-century creativity? 'Designer' in the literal sense: today's top pastry chefs sketch out their ideas, produce seasonal collections and present them. Cakes are indeed the stuff of dreams at the **Pâtisserie des Rêves**, where Philippe Contacini's creations are displayed like jewels under a pyramid of gleaming glass cloches. Gems include a Saint-Honoré with caramel and an artistic wave of cream, a chocolate eclair that sits within a tube of chocolate and a flower-shaped Paris-Brest. Around the corner at **Hugo & Victor**, inspiration comes in a more literary form, with a black glass and chrome interior and chocolate boxes that look like books. Pastry chef Hugues Pouget works with eight key flavours: chocolate, vanilla and caramel year round along with five changing, seasonal flavours. Each features in glossy marble-like chocolates and two gâteaux – experimental Hugo and more classic Victor – along with a wine suggestion to match each flavour group.

Want to make your cake part of a chic picnic? **La Grande Epicerie**, the food hall of Bon Marché department store, is a favourite with ladies who shop, particularly noted for its Italian deli counter.

*Pâtisserie des Rêves; 93 rue du Bac; tel: 01 42 84 00 82; www.lapatisserie desreves.com; Tue–Sat 9am–8pm, Sun 9am–4pm; map D5*
*Hugo & Victor; 40 Boulevard Raspail; tel: 01 44 39 97 73; www.hugovictor. com; Mon–Sat 9am–8.15pm, Sun 9am–1.30pm; map D5*
*La Grande Epicerie; 38 rue de Sèvres; tel: 01 44 39 81 00; www.lagrande epicerie.fr; Mon–Sat 8.30am–9pm; map D5*

# **Feast** with the foodies on **rue St-Dominique**

In the Paris of embassies, ministries and old money, smart residents and civil servants like to eat well, and rue St-Dominique could almost be renamed Christian Constant Street. After being chef at Le Crillon, Constant opened elegant bistro **Le Violon d'Ingres** (No. 135; tel: 01 45 55 15 05). Since then he has added **Café Constant** (No. 139), an all-day, no-reservation, café-bistro, where you can come to read the paper over coffee or a meal; and **Les Cocottes** (No. 135), his stylish take on a casual diner where the concept is grandmotherly home cooking, slow-baked in *cocottes* (cast-iron casserole dishes).

A little further on, overlooking a fountain on a small arcaded square, **La Fontaine de Mars** (*pictured*; No. 129; tel: 01 47 05 46 44) is all red and white check tablecloths and old apéritif posters. Renowned for its raditional southwestern specialities, it was propelled into the spotlight when Barrack Obama dined here with his family.

Another former Crillon chef, Jean-François Piège recently revived vintage brasserie **Thoumieux** (No. 79; tel: 01 47 05 79 79). Downstairs it's classy brasserie, upstairs, gourmet **Restaurant de Jean-François Piège**, with just 20 seats in a neo-50s decor that smacks of being invited round to someone's apartment. Choose from five key ingredients as the basis for a selection of inventive dishes.

Around the corner, **L'Ami Jean** (27 rue Malar; tel: 01 47 05 86 89) is a leader of the *bistronomique* trend – read gastronomic food in a bistro atmosphere at economical prices – a raucous Basque tavern setting for Stéphane Jego's generous, lovely dishes served to a clientele of rugby fans and foodies.

*Rue St-Dominique; map B6*

143

# Relive **artistic Montparnasse** through its **classic brasseries**

Montparnasse's artistic and intellectual heyday can almost be spelled out by the string of brasseries along its boulevard, once a home from home to a roll call of artists and writers who epitomised the dynamic age of modern art, jazz and cocktails, and the international melting-pot of the Ecole de Paris – Italian Modigliani, later the Surrealists Picasso and Cocteau, American photographer Man Ray. Modern development has taken its toll on the boulevard, but there's still some wonderful people-watching of oyster eaters and cinema goers to be had.

When **La Coupôle** (*pictured*; 118 boulevard du Montparnasse; tel: 01 43 20 14 20) opened in 1927, it was the city's largest restaurant, with columns painted by different artists, art deco lights and mosaics, and basement 'dansing' where couples danced the sexy new tango imported from Argentina. You can sit in the window for a drink or inside at white-napped tables for oysters, shellfish, or its unexpected house speciality of lamb curry. **Le Select** (No. 99; tel: 01 45 48 38 14), across the street, still has the aura of a speakeasy and a sign proclaiming 'bar américain'; **La Rotonde** (No. 105; tel: 01 43 26 48 26), opened in 1911, is a cocoon of brass and red velvet; and **Le Dôme** (No. 108; tel: 01 43 35 25 81) has become a luxury fish restaurant. But something of the old spirit survives at **Le Rosebud** (11 bis rue Delambre; tel: 01 43 35 38 54), a cocktail bar that never quite fades from fashion. Further along the boulevard, **La Closerie des Lilas** (No. 171; tel: 01 40 51 34 50) is still favoured by writers and politicians. Get in the mood over a cocktail in the piano bar, as you sit at a table where a brass plaque might just indicate that Hemingway, Trotsky or Picasso sat there before you.

*Boulevard du Montparnasse; map D-E3*

# Descend 130 steps under Paris to its **skeletal foundations**: the macabre world of **the Catacombes**

'Stop, this is the Empire of death!' sets the tone for the philosophical musings that accompany you around the **Catacombes de Paris**, reached after a descent down 130 steps and a walk along a tunnel that takes you through a section of the labyrinth of quarries dug out since Roman times – like a veritable gruyère cheese under the city – passing on the way an extraordinary sculpture of Fort Mahon in Majorca.

The Catacombes, or 'municipal ossuary', was created in the late 18th century when the city's overcrowded, malodorous and unhygienic cemeteries were cleared out and, between 1786 and 1860, the bones of some six million Parisians transferred here. But it was in 1810 that Héricart de Thury, inspector general of the quarries, had the idea of putting the bones in neat formations, arranging them in the incredibly neat piles of long bones with bands of skulls, sometimes in great circular sweeps, that make the Catacombes a setting for reflecting on death, memory and the fragility of human life. Plaques listing the cemetery the remains were taken from and the date, along with macabre quotations by writers and philosophers such as Lamartine and Molière, complete the picture.

The Catacombes were opened to visitors almost as soon as they were created and, as well as some illustrious official visitors, Napoleon III included, have ever since also attracted urban myths and illicit party-goers (often not in the catacombs themselves but in the parts of other quarries located around the city).

Bring a jumper if you visit in summer – the quarries are a chilly 14°C all year round.

*Les Catacombes de Paris; 1 avenue du Colonel Rol-Tanguy, place Denfert-Rochereau; tel: 01 43 22 47 63; www. catacombes.paris.fr; Tue–Sun 10am–5pm, last entrance 4pm; charge; map E1*

# Dredge under the capital for an insight into its inner workings: the labyrinthine **Paris sewers**

A walk around the **Egouts de Paris** is probably the only chance most of us will ever have of visiting a sewer – an educational insight into the underground workings of a great city and the ebb and flow of its water and effluents. Although it's often billed as a children's attraction, it's more of a sub-urban trip around the entrails of the city, testimony to the less visible engineering prowess behind the capital's 19th-century expansion. Blue enamel signs announcing avenue Bosquet or rue Cognacq-Jay mirror those labelling the streets up above so that sewer workers can know exactly where they are. The tour takes in just a tiny proportion of the 2,400km (1,490 miles) of dank

galleries under the capital, as you walk past canals and channels, sluices and pumps, accompanied by the constant sound of rushing water, and an array of dredging barges and machines to keep everything flowing. Panels describe the history of the sewers, from the very first covered sewer (before which there were only open drains) on rue Montmartre in 1370, during the reign of Charles V. In the 1850s, Baron Haussmann's chief engineer, Eugène Belgrand, masterminded the creation of today's sewage and water distribution system, a system not just about sewage but also about providing drinking water to Parisians, drainage and the control of flood water. It involved a sewer in every street, forming a complex web as small sewers flowed into successively larger channels, and a double water supply sytem, providing drinking water for homes and non-drinking water to clean the streets.

*Egouts de Paris;, Pont de l'Alma, Left Bank, facing 93 quai d'Orsay; tel: 01 53 68 27 81; www.paris.fr; May–Sept Sat–Wed 11am–5pm, Oct–Apr Sat–Wed 11am–4pm, closed 25 Dec–1 Jan and 2 weeks in Jan; charge; map B7*

# Be a fly on the wall in an early 20th-century **artist's studio in Montparnasse**

Today Antoine Bourdelle is chiefly remembered as a creator of muscular Modernist sculptures and, in an obscure art historical link, as assistant of Rodin and teacher of Giacometti. However, small **Musée Bourdelle,** centred around Bourdelle's old studio and family apartment, also offers a vision of artists' Montparnasse at the start of the 20th century. Several large works, including figures for Bourdelle's equestrian monument to Argentine general Alvéar, are displayed in the garden and a 1960s extension; while a new wing contains some of the countless busts of Beethoven through which, like Rodin with Balzac, Bourdelle explored tortured, creative genius and endlessly worked through different moods and character traits. But the most atmospheric part of the museum is the overgrown row

of dusty artists' studios, where Bourdelle had his atelier from 1885 until his death in 1929. Happily, it hasn't been too tidied up.

*Musée Bourdelle, 18 rue Antoine-Bourdelle; tel: 01 49 54 73 73; www.paris. fr, Tue–Sun 10am–6pm; free, charge during exhibitions; map C3*

---

**MONTPARNASSE ARTISTS' TRAIL**
**Musée du Montparnasse** (21 avenue du Maine; tel: 01 42 22 91 96; www.museedumontparnasse.net). In the atelier where Russian artist Marie Vassilieff ran an art academy and canteen and threw exotic parties.
**Musée Zadkine** (100 bis rue d'Assas; tel: 01 43 26 91 90; www.paris.fr). The house and studio of the Russian-born sculptor and wife Valentine Prax.
**Fondation Henri Cartier-Bresson** (2 impasse Lebouis; tel: 01 56 80 27 00; www.henricartierbresson.org). The studio house now contains Cartier-Bresson's archives and presents shows of his work and other photographers.

## Beyond the Centre

# Beyond the Centre

0    1    2    3 km

0    1        2 miles

A86

GENNEVILLIERS

Avenue Louis Roche

Île des
Vannes

BOIS-
COLOMBES

ASNIÈRES-
SUR-SEINE

Cimetière des
Chiens

SAINT-OUEN

LA GARENNE-
COLOMBES

PORT DE CLICHY

CLICHY

Puces de
St-Ouen

COURBEVOIE

Île de
Grande Jatte

LEVALLOIS-
PERRET

ÉPINETTES

18ᵉ

NANTERRE

LA
DÉFENSE

PUTEAUX

NEUILLY-
SUR-SEINE

TERNES

17ᵉ

MONTMARTRE

SURESNES

JARDIN
D'ACCLIMATATION

Île de
Puteaux

Arc de
Triomphe

Gare
St-Lazare

9ᵉ

8ᵉ

Lac
Inférieur

CHAILLOT

Grand
Palais

Petit
Palais

Musée du
Louvre

BOIS DE
BOULOGNE

Musée Marmottan Monet
La Gare

Tour Eiffel

Musée
d'Ursay

Hippodrome
de Longchamp

Hippodrome
d'Auteuil

Fondation
Hippocrène

Fondation
Le Corbusier

16ᵉ

Hôtel des
Invalides

Palais du
Luxembourg

Panthéo

AUTEUIL

JARDIN DES
SERRES
D'AUTEUIL

GRENELLE

15ᵉ

Tour
Montparnasse

Gare
Montparnasse

BOULOGNE-
BILLANCOURT

DOMAINE
NATIONAL DE
ST-CLOUD

Musée National
de la Céramique

PARC
GEORGES
BRASSENS

14ᵉ

SÈVRES

Île Seguin

Île de
Ste-Germain

ISSY-LES-
MOULINEAUX

VANVES

PARC
MONTSOURIS

Cité
Internationale
Universitaire

MALAKOFF

MONTROUGE

Orly

A              B              C              D

# Be amazed by the largest collection of Monets in the world at **Musée Marmottan Monet**

Poised in upmarket residential Paris, **Musée Marmottan** is a dignified Second Empire villa where you just happen to find the largest collection of works by Claude Monet in the world. Many of them were bequeathed by Monet's son Michel, and you can follow all the stages of the artist's oeuvre including *Impression, Soleil Levant* – the pink-skied view of the port at Le Havre that gave its name to the Impressionist movement – rare caricatures, early landscapes and portraits of his children, sketchbooks and the artist's palette too. The holy of holies is the circular basement room hung with a series of vibrantly coloured paintings of Monet's water garden at Giverny *(see also Musée de l'Orangerie, p.54)*. Monet created the garden with an eye to painting it, as a growing artwork in its own right, selecting plants and creating viewpoints and patches of light and shadow. And here, amid the

rich blues and viridian green, are glimpses and reflections of water lilies, weeping willows, the Japanese bridge and the punt moored to the bank. The museum also has other fine Impressionist works by Caillebotte, Sisley, Manet and Pissarro, and several of Berthe Morisot's tender paintings of children.

The house, conveniently close to the Bois de Boulogne, was originally the hunting pavilion of the Duke de Valmy. It was later extended by Paul Marmottan, who filled it with an exceptional collection of First Empire furniture, much of it resplendent with Egyptian motifs and sphinxes, that he left to the state, and an unusual clock in Sèvres porcelain which tells the time in twelve cities around the world.

*Musée Marmottan Monet, 2 rue Louis-Boilly; tel: 01 44 96 50 33; www. marmottan.com; Tue–Sun 10am–6pm, Thur until 8pm; charge; map B2*

# Stand in the **home of Modernity**: avant-garde icons by **Le Corbusier** in Auteuil

If you're interested in modern architecture, then adjoining Villas La Roche and Jeanneret (now **Fondation Le Corbusier**), built 1923–25, are fascinating. Here, in the small but clever building full of light and interesting views, you can see Le Corbusier putting his ideas into practice early in his career, using reinforced concrete in what would become his celebrated five principles of architecture: pilottis, strip windows, open-plan spaces, roof terraces and ingenious built-in furniture, intended to meet all the needs of modern living. This is no modern white box. If the outside is all crisp and white, inside the architect experimented with colours on certain walls to alter the perception of volumes.

For all its staid image today, plush Auteuil boasted plenty of adventurous patrons in the 1920s. One street away, almost all of rue Mallet-Stevens was designed by

Robert Mallet-Stevens, the elegant dandy of the Modern Movement. His own architectural offices now belong to the **Fondation Hippocrène**, which supports European artists and writers and is open for exhibitions and events – a chance to admire its Cubist volumes and characteristic use of iron and glass.

> **MORE LE CORBUSIER IN PARIS**
> Other Paris buildings by the architect include the Molitor apartment block, where you can visit Le Corbusier's apartment and architectural studio (24 rue Nungessor et Coli; tel: 01 42 88 75 72, Sat); and two blocks at the Cité Universitaire (see p.162) and the Armée du Salut hostel (*pictured*; rue Cantagrel).

*Fondation Le Corbusier, 10 square du Dr Blanche; tel: 01 42 88 75 72; www.fondationlecorbusier.fr; Mon 1.30–6pm, Tue–Thur 10–6pm, Fri–Sat 10am–5pm, closed 1–7 Aug; charge; map B2*
*Fondation Hippocrène, 12 rue Mallet-Stevens; tel 01 45 20 95 94; www.fondation-hippocrene.fr; during exhibitions Mon–Sat 1.30–7pm; map B2*

Get on the **nature trail** along **La Petite Ceinture**, a green belt along the tracks of a disused railway

Unlike the manicured look of Parisian parks, **La Petite Ceinture** nature trail between Gare d'Auteuil and La Muette (rue de Ranelagh) is a cheerfully overgrown tangle of grass and bushes, a wonderful vision of the town reconquered by nature on the embankments and former tracks of the Petite Ceinture (little belt) railway that once encircled Paris. Panels point out the different habitats – meadow, woodland, scrub with bushes, clematis and honeysuckle, wetland with willows, limestone spur and the cutting wall colonised by ferns and creepers – surrounded only by birdsong from tits, warblers and woodpeckers. At the end of the promenade, the red brick Passy-La Muette station has been converted into **La Gare** (19 chaussée de la Muette; tel: 01 42 15 15 31; www. restaurantlagare.com), a stylish restaurant with tables spread out along the platforms, and a bar set in the former ticket office.

The 32km (20-mile) – long railway was built between 1852 and 1869 to connect the different main lines, first to carry goods, later transporting Parisians as a forerunner of the Métro. The line closed to passenger trains in 1934 (it continued for freight until 1993), but still fascinates, with fans who

campaign for its preservation. You can glimpse traces of it all over town: cuttings as you walk in Parc Montsouris and Parc des Buttes-Chaumont, a tunnel under Parc Georges Brassens, lone railway bridges or remaining stations such as the Gare de Charonne, now the Flèche d'Or (*p.159*).

Another short section has been turned into a nature trail and community garden in the 12th *arrondissement*, reached from square Charles Péguy, where it joins the **Promenade Plantée** (along the disused Bastille–Vincennes line); and a new footpath will follow in the 15th *arrondissement*, bringing a touch of wilderness between rue St-Charles and rue Olivier de Serres.

*La Petite Ceinture nature trail; map B2 and E-F2*

# Let off steam in the lushly romantic, 19th-century hothouses of **Les Serres d'Auteuil**

**Les Serres d'Auteuil**, also known as 'the municipal florist', is an extraordinary ensemble of romantic, 19th-century bluey-green iron greenhouses centred around the Grande Serre, a steamy palm house where you find yourself engulfed in jungle amid giant palms, pools of brooding ornamental carp and an aviary of chatty tropical birds. Part of the appeal of the genteely shabby *serres* (greenhouses) is that they aren't so much about putting on a public display as being fully working greenhouses – originally providing plants for municipal parks and squares, now cultivating heritage collections. A few informative labels are dotted around, including a discussion on the likelihood of plant indigestion when a carnivorous plant has eaten too many insects. Sadly, part of the site is under threat from the expansion of the Roland Garros tennis courts next door, home to France's grand slam tournament.

In summer, the Azalea Pavilion is a romantic setting for concerts as part of **Solistes aux Serres d'Auteuil** (tel: 01 46 32 02 26; www.ars-mobilis.com), when a grand piano is installed under the glass roof, making the most of its remarkably good acoustics.

The gardens are unfortunately hemmed in by a junction of the Périphérique ring road. Beyond stretches the Bois de Boulogne, an expanse of wood and parkland crossed by too many roads whose facilities range from elitist private sports clubs and gastronomic restaurants to a large campsite. The best part is the Lac Inférieur, where you can hire boats in summer and row out to a small island.

*Jardin des Serres d'Auteuil; 1 avenue Gordon-Bennett; daily 10am–6pm, winter until 5pm; free. Summer concerts: tel: 01 46 32 02 26; www.ars-mobilis.com; charge; map B2*

# Learn about satellites at **La Villette**: a day at the Cité des Sciences, Cité de la Musique and modern park

With the **Cité des Sciences** on one side, **Cité de la Musique** on the other and the Parc de la Villette stretching between the two, La Villette was part of a vast transformation project started in the 1980s to revive this corner of northwest Paris, site of the old abattoirs and livestock market. As urban renewal, it's done pretty well. During the school holidays, it swarms with children and seethes with activities, though it's a long way from images of romantic Paris – perhaps more like a grown-up theme park (minus people dressed up as mice). You can see films in the spherical mirrored **Géode** IMAX cinema (*pictured*), go round the **Argonaute**, a 1950s submarine, follow an undulating path along the Canal de l'Ourcq, which cuts through the centre of the park, explore themed gardens, and go to rock concerts or jazz festivals.

The **Cité des Sciences et de l'Industrie,** a hi-tech science museum, has all the expected hands-on explanations of sound, light, images and mathematics, while other sections look more at technology's effect on modern life, with energy and transport examined for instance. When it comes to satellites, the idea is not so much us looking up at space but how satellites look down on us, surveying both where we are and the state of the planet.

Outside, 26 red metal structures or '*folies*', designed by Swiss architect Bernard Tschumi, dot the park like points on a grid, serving various functions including burger bar, information kiosk, bandstand and first aid post. Across the Canal St-Martin, a serpentine path leads through a trail of themed gardens designed by artists and architects, with bamboo plants and Buren's pebble stripes, Fabrice Hyber's anti-memorial for Aids, vines and fountains, spooky noises, and a dune garden with trampolines and pedal windmills for small children.

Perhaps the best time of all to appreciate the park is during the **Cinéma en Plein Air** (mid July– mid Aug) outdoor film festival, when you can relax on the lawn and watch great movies projected on a giant screen at nightfall.

A few relics of the old livestock market remain: the **Grande Halle**, the **Théâtre Paris-Villette** and the former vets' pavilion now restored as the **WIP Villette**, dedicated to hip hop and street art. Next to the Grande Halle, the wedge-shaped **Cité de la Musique** is both a concert hall and a music museum. Musical instruments, such as Chopin's Pleyel grand piano, Stradivarius violins, beautiful harpsichords, serpents, synthesizers and Algerian lutes are displayed amid paintings and sculpture to put them in context, and you might come across mini recitals as you walk around. This is one place where the audioguide truly makes a difference, playing the sound of some of the instruments on display and extracts of music ranging from Scarlatti, Offenbach and Dowland to a Hammond organ. The concert hall is a clever, modulable space putting on an incredibly broad range of music, from early music and symphonies to Arab music.

There are cafés and places to eat around the park, but for a taste of the old meat traders' Villette, indulge in a humongous steak at **Au Boeuf Couronné** (188 avenue Jean-Jaurès; tel: 01 42 39 44 44), a survivor of the market brasseries opposite the park.

*Cité de la Musique; 221 avenue Jean-Jaurès; tel: 01 44 84 44 84; www. citedelamusique.fr; Tue–Sat noon– 6pm, Sun 10am–6pm, concert times vary; charge; map F4*

*Cité des Sciences et de l'Industrie; 30 avenue Corentin-Cariou; tel: 01 40 05 80 00; www.cite-sciences.fr; Tue–Sat 10am–6pm, Sun 10am–7pm; charge; map F4*

*Parc de la Villette; www.villette. com; daily 24 hours; free; map F4*

# Attend an open studio or shop for organic goodies at municipal undertaker's turned art space the **104**

The echoing halls of the **CentQuatre** (104) resound to dance steps and video installations – not bad for a place that used to be the municipal undertaker's. In its time, the vast neoclassical building contained stabling for 2,000 horses, storerooms and workshops for making coffins and hearses. After closing in 1998, it was refurbished as a complex of artists' studios, rehearsal rooms and performance spaces set around a glazed central hall conceived as an internal street – open, if windswept, to visitors and local inhabitants.

The approach is multidisciplinary so that at any one time residents might include artists, musicians, theatre directors, choreographers, DJs or landscape designers. All open their studios to the public on a regular basis, although, as this is considered a place for creation rather than presentation, there may not be much to see when you visit. A programme of exhibitions, concerts and performances, children's workshops and Friday night urban dance sessions offer other alternatives. Events in the Halle d'Aubervilliers have included a clanking merry-go-round of articulated elephants, buffalo and insects, which entranced children and adults for six months in 2011.

On one side, restaurant **Les Grandes Tables** (tel: 01 40 37 10 07) has given the area a culinary boost, while The **Emmaüs** charity shop (Wed–Sat) breathes new life into furniture and objects, a business incubator is being set up, and there's an organic food market on Saturdays. After a slow start, the CentQuatre is definitely finding its place in the Paris cultural scene.

*Le CentQuatre; 5 rue Curial or 104 rue d'Aubervilliers; tel: 01 54 35 50 00; www.104.fr; Tue–Sun 11am–8pm, closed 2 weeks in Aug; exhibitions free, performances charge; map E4*

158

# Chill out in villagey **Charonne**

Northeast Paris gives a taste of the old working-class Paris, offering a sometimes slightly schizoid mix of picturesque villagey remnants and 1970s tower-block horrors.

The square-towered **Eglise St-Germain-de-Charonne**, dating from the 12th to the 15th centuries, still forms the heart of old village Charonne, with its cemetery climbing up the hill behind it. Opposite the church, pedestrianised rue St-Blaise, once the village high street, has a bucolic air, with its ateliers and bistros – try **Café Noir** (No. 15; tel: 01 40 09 75 80) for a meal – and little gardens. Prettily renovated Square des Grès, once the site of a pillory, stands as an unlikely crossroads between gentrification and a vast public housing estate.

Trendy hotel/restaurant **Mama Shelter** (109 rue de Bagnolet; tel: 01 43 48 48 48; www.mamashelter. com), designed by Philippe Starck, confirms the area's ascent in fashion terms, with a concrete-chic restaurant, cocktail bar and DJs at weekends, as well as outdoor tables overlooking the Petite Ceinture (*p.154*). Charonne's former train station is now the **Flèche d'Or** (No. 102 bis; tel: 01 44 64 01 02; www. flechedor.fr) music venue.

In a small park up the street is the **Pavillon de l'Ermitage** (*pictured*; 148 rue de Bagnolet; tel: 01 40 24 15 95; www. pavillondelermitage.com; Mar– July, Sept–mid-Dec Fri–Sat 2–7pm; charge), a rococo summer house built for 'Madame', the daughter of Louis XIV and Madame de Montespan, in the grounds of the long-gone Domaine de Bagnolet back when the gentry had their country retreats in the area.

Minutes away is what estate agents today refer to as 'the countryside comes to Paris': the streets of tightly packed, creeper-covered houses and stairways around rue Mondonville, rue Jules Siegfried and rue Irénée Blanc, built for the labourers at the local gypsum quarries of yore.

*Charonne; map F2*

# Discover **global Paris** at the **Cité de l'Immigration**

By an ironic twist of history, the Palais de la Porte Dorée constructed for the 1931 Colonial Exhibition, has become a centre recounting the history of two centuries of immigration to France. Documents, artefacts, archive photos, artworks and sound recordings explore the breadth of the subject. Immigration has not just been from the former colonies in West and North Africa and from Southeast Asia, but has also seen Polish miners come to the north of France, Italian labourers, Eastern European Jews prior to World War II, white Russians and refugees from the Spanish Civil War. What brings these histories alive are the individual stories, told via personal recordings or through the donated items particularly significant of past and new lives: photos, a school certificate, battered suitcases, a sewing machine. Some striking modern art includes Barthélémy Toguo's witty six-high stack of bunk beds, weighed under by the characteristic checked carrier bags of immigrants in an over-crowded migrant workers' hostel.

The building is a fabulous piece of 1930s architecture, with a sweeping colonnaded facade covered with reliefs of pith-hatted hunters, jungle beasts and palm trees, and redolent of colonialism, a frescoed Salle des Fêtes, and two superb Art Deco offices still with their original zebra wood furniture designed by Eugène Printz and Emile-Jacques Ruhlmann. The basement contains another relic of 1931 – the enormously popular aquarium, originally intended to introduce the French public to the marine life of its colonies. It is always awash with colourful fish and children, watching to see if the inhabitants of the crocodile pit will pounce. The last of the Nile crocodiles brought here in 1948 recently died and been replaced by four Mississippi alligators.

*Cité de l'Immigration; 293 avenue Daumesnil; tel: 01 53 59 58 60; www.histoire-immigration.fr; www.aquarium-portedoree.fr; Tue–Fri 10am–5.30pm, Sat, Sun 10am–7pm; charge; map F1*

# Chinatown

The tower blocks of the 13th *arrondissement* don't look too prepossessing at first glance, but Paris's largest Chinatown, concentrated along avenue d'Ivry and avenue de Choisy, has an identity all its own, with the crowds and businesses giving it an invigorating feel of Hong Kong.

Life centres around the two enormous supermarkets, **Tang Frères** (48 avenue d'Ivry) and **Paris Store** (44 avenue d'Ivry), filled with mangosteens and dragon fruit, noodles and wonton wrappers, obscure sweets and jellies, not to mention departments devoted to cooking pots, porcelain and plastic flowers. Above the street, on the esplanade of the **Olympiades** shopping centre, a line of pagoda-shaped pavilions is apparently a happy coincidence – built to attract middle-class residents but colonised instead by Asian immigrants and now containing Asian restaurants. Many of the restaurants here are pan-Asian, serving a mixture of Chinese, Vietnamese, Laotian and Thai dishes. Go to **Pho 14** (129 avenue de Choisy; tel: 01 45 83 61 15) for an authentic formica-style Vietnamese eatery, always busy with diners slurping *pho* soup – a broth thick with rice noodles and topped with pork, meatballs or slices of beef, into which you add beansprouts and mint leaves. **Lao Lane Xang 2** (102 avenue d'Ivry; tel: 01 58 89 00 00) is known for its Laotian and Thai dishes with a simpler sibling establishment across the street at No. 105.

There is more to Chinatown than slurping noodles however. Off avenue d'Ivry, just as rue du Disque appears to descend into an underground car park, a few steps bring you to the **Autel du Culte Bouddhiste**, where amid dangling red lanterns and the smell of incense, people place offerings of fruit, rice or cooking oil before small altars – it's like you've really been transported to Asia.

*Chinatown; map E1*

# Play detective at the **Cité Internationale** student campus – the clue's in the architecture

Created in a spirit of international goodwill after World War I, the **Cité Internationale Universitaire** is a sort of United Nations of students, modelled on Oxbridge colleges and American university campuses, home to 5,000 students and visiting academics from around the world. The 37 halls of residence spread around a park were built in the styles of different countries, sometimes in a pastiche of vernacular styles, making for an amusing architectural guessing game: a classical pediment for the **Fondation Hellénique**, bird-beaked gables on the **Maison du Cambodge**, a Moorish-tiled entrance appended onto the **Maison du Maroc**. Le Corbusier designed two pavilions: the **Fondation Suisse**, in 1933, where you can visit the curved salon with its colourful mural and a bedroom furnished by Charlotte Perriand, and the **Maison du Brésil**, in 1959 – very similar to his Cités Radieuses

in Marseille, Firminy and Nantes with its long, raw concrete facade and red, yellow or green balconies, and self-contained with theatre, canteen and library. The central **Maison Internationale** (*pictured*), American-designed but inspired by French châteaux, holds the **Théâtre de la Cité Internationale** (tel: 01 43 13 50 50), which puts on some first-rate modern dance. The Cité is still growing, with a positive-energy Maison de France building due to open in 2014.

Cross boulevard Jourdain to come to **Parc Montsouris**, one of Napoleon III's picturesque parks.

*Cité Internationale Universitaire de Paris; 17 boulevard Jourdain; tel: 01 44 16 64 00; www.ciup.fr; map D1 Fondation Suisse; tel: 01 44 16 10 16; www.fondationsuisse.fr; daily 10am–noon, 2–5pm; charge; map D1 Maison du Brésil; tel: 01 58 10 23 00; www.maisondubresil.org; daily 8am–noon, 1–8pm; charge; map D1*

# Go on a treasure hunt at the **Puces de St-Ouen**, Paris's **biggest flea market**

Described as the largest antiques market in the world, the location of the **Puces de St-Ouen** harks back to the days when rag-and-bone men were allowed to sell goods, free of duty, just outside the city walls. Today it has been listed for its unique style and character, a lure for thousands of visitors each weekend. However, to describe the Puces de St-Ouen as a market hardly gives you an idea of its scale: over 2,500 individual dealers spread across more than a dozen markets, most of them strung along the rue des Rosiers. There's everything, from classy antiques to incredible junk, and an ever-growing fashion for modern design and collectables.

**Marché Vernaison** is atmospheric and eclectic, the oldest and most flea of the markets, encompassing 300 stalls in a triangle of alleys. Hidden in its depths, touristy but fun *bistro-chansonnier* **Chez Louisette** serves mussels and chips while singers belt out Piaf. Nearby **Marché Biron** is mainly devoted to period antiques for those with a taste for ormolu and chandeliers.

**Marché Dauphine**, purpose-built in the 1990s, has plenty of high-quality goods, with antique mirrors and barometers at Leda, 19th-century aperitif sets, carpets, paintings, toys and watches. Take an escalator to the first floor for vintage clothes, books and postcards. **Marché Serpette** is indoors and rather chic, where you might find historic panelling, Art Deco furniture and wonderful costume jewellery at Olwen Forest. Stallholders set out tables for lunch and play chess between visitors. **Marché Paul Bert**, which runs round the sides, is a decorators' favourite, with eclectic furniture, garden statuary, great kitchenwares specialist Bachelier and lots of 20th-century design.

There are plenty of bars and bistros, and should your purchase be too big to get into a suitcase, transporter and shipping company representatives are on the spot.

*Puces de St-Ouen, St-Ouen; Sat–Mon 8am–6pm; map D4*

# Pay homage to man's best friend – and Kiki the monkey – at the **Cimetière des Chiens**

Cocotte the hen and assorted budgerigars and hamsters.

Facing the entrance is a grand monument to Barry, the Saint Bernard, with a sculpture of a small child riding on the back of a mountain rescue dog: 'He saved the life of 40 people. He was killed by the 41st'. Then there are a few stars such as Rin Tin Tin, the Alsatian who starred in numerous Hollywood films in the 1920s and 30s, an endless cast of Mimis and Mitzis, Rexes, Pompoms, Loulous, Betsy and Oscars, and a living population of stray cats sleeping on the gravestones.

It helps if you can read a little French to make the most of the moving epitaphs, messages to faithful companions and tales of lonely lives – 'Disappointed by humans, never by my dog' is one. And amidst it all, there are perhaps a few happy endings too, as in: 'On the 15th May 1958 was buried here the errant dog who died at the gates of the cemetery and was the 40,000th beast to find eternal rest in Asnières dog cemetery.'

Bordering the Seine at Asnières-sur-Seine, the dog cemetery is a moving shrine to much-loved pets. The oldest pet cemetery in the world was opened in 1899 by militant feminist journalist Marguerite Durand and lawyer Georges Harmois, who bought the site on the Ile des Ravageurs (now no longer quite an island as the channel has been filled in). Architect Eugène Petit designed a grandiose entrance in a mix of Art Nouveau and Moorish styles, gateway to the gravestones not just of dogs but lots of cats, a racehorse or two, Kiki the monkey,

*Cimetière des Chiens; 4 Pont de Clichy, Asnières-sur-Seine; tel: 01 40 86 21 11; www.asnieres-sur-seine.fr; Tue-Sun 10am-6pm, winter until 4.30pm; charge; map C4*

# Frequent the royals at the **Basilique St-Denis**

One thousand years ago, the suburb of St-Denis, north of Paris, had a very different image to the one it has today. Then it was considered a sacred spot, a place of pilgrimage ever since early Christian martyr Denis had ended up here – carrying his head, which had been chopped off in Montmartre. Today, the magnificent Gothic **basilica** comes as a surprise amid the modern multicultural suburb, home to the remains of docks and premises from its Industrial Age heyday.

Begun in the 12th century over an earlier church, the basilica is considered the first true Gothic structure with its ogival vaulting and rose window. It is particularly lovely for classical concerts every June during the Festival St-Denis but, above all, it is fascinating as the burial place of French monarchy. In the crypt are traces of the Carolingian church and a 12th-century crypt, where the remains of Louis XVI, Marie Antoinette and the last of the Bourbons are buried.

St-Denis's other landmark is the **Stade de France**, constructed just in time for France's victory in the 1998 World Cup, and instantly recognisable with its flying-saucer roof. You can tour the stadium, visiting the stands and changing rooms and running out onto the pitch through the players' tunnel.

*Basilique St-Denis; 1 rue de la Légion d'Honneur; tel: 01 48 09 83 54; www.saint-denis.monuments-nationaux.fr; Mon–Sat 10am–6.15pm, Sun noon–6.15pm, winter until 5.15pm); nave free, charge for tombs; map E5*
*Stade de France, St-Denis; tel: 08 92 70 09 00; www.stadefrance.com; guided visits, times vary; charge; map E5*

# Picnic in the **Domaine de St-Cloud** with superb views of Paris across the Seine

Vistas and terraces, formal gardens and, above all, large expanses of grass and woodland make the **Domaine de St-Cloud** one of the loveliest places for a weekend stroll or a summer picnic, among the magnificent remains of a grand château park (minus the château, which burned down in 1870). Once the property of 'Monsieur' – Philippe d'Orléans, brother of Louis XIV, the park, – landscaped by André Le Nôtre, the king's master gardener, also responsible for Versailles and the Tuileries – became a favourite setting for grand fêtes given by 19th-century royalty. There's a superb view of Paris across the Seine from the belvedere, and a network of fountains to rival Versailles are put into action on Sunday afternoons, May and June. There are cafés, a small farm, a circus pitch and pedal cars, a grand firework spectacular in September, and one of France's best rock festivals, Rock en Seine, on the last weekend in August.

At the foot of the park is the Manufacture de Sèvres, the historic porcelain factory founded in the 18th century which still makes porcelain to historic designs from its archives (visits of the ateliers by rendezvous). Recently rebaptised Sèvres, Cité de la Céramique, the 25 listed buildings also include the **Musée National de la Céramique**, presenting a huge panorama of ceramics from around the world.

*Domaine Nationale de St-Cloud; St-Cloud; www.saint-cloud.monuments-nationaux.fr; daily summer 7.30am–9/10pm, winter 7.30am–8pm; charge for cars; map A1*

*Musée National de Sèvres; 2 place de la Manufacture, Sèvres; tel: 01 46 29 22 00; www.sevresciteceramique.fr; Wed–Mon 10am–5pm; charge; map A1*

# Climb a medieval skyscraper in **Vincennes**, then lie back to the sound of **music in the park**

Compared to the Louvre or Versailles, the one-time role of the **Château de Vincennes** as royal residence has been rather forgotten; but its recently restored donjon (keep) – at 50 metres (164ft) high, the tallest in France – imparts a vision of Charles V's ambition when he moved out of Ile de la Cité and turned a secondary residence of the Capetians into a powerful stronghold. After climbing the surrounding *châtelet*, where you can admire the view from the parapet walk, a bridge brings you to the keep, where Charles V's council room, with its vaulted ceiling and three metre (10ft) – thick walls, and the royal chamber up above, give a surprising sense of medieval palace life. Charles V also built the curtain wall (big enough to contain an entire town), and began the Ste Chapelle, a soaring Gothic edifice. The castle continued to be used by the monarchy, especially when things got too hot in Paris.

If you're here on a summer weekend, combine your visit with a concert in the **Parc Floral**, across the esplanade to the south. An excellent line up of jazz musicians in the **Paris Jazz Festival** (www.parisjazzfestival.fr) in June–July gives way to symphony orchestras and chamber music in **Classique au Vert** (www.classiqueauvert.fr) in August–September. There are some seats by the stage but most people laze on the lawns or lounge between flowerbeds across the lake. This modern botanical garden re-creates different habitats – pinewood, oak forest, water lily pond, butterfly house, bonsai garden – as well as an amusing minigolf around the monuments of Paris.

*Château de Vincennes; avenue de Paris, Vincennes; tel: 01 43 28 15 48; www.vincennes.monuments-nationaux.fr; daily Apr–Sept 10am–6.15pm, Oct–Mar 10am–5.15pm; charge; map G2*
*Parc Floral de Paris; Bois de Vincennes; daily summer 9am–8/9pm, winter 9am–5pm; free except charge Wed, Sat, Sun June–Sept; map G2*

# hotels

Parisian hotels are like snapshots of the city itself, inserted in the urban fabric and echoing the character of the different *quartiers*.

Beyond the legendary grand palace hotels, where you can expect palatial bedrooms, squadrons of staff able to meet every whim, sybaritic spas and gourmet restaurants, accommodation-wise the Parisian norm is still the small privately run hotel. Many are in historic buildings, where ancient beams, exposed stone walls and breakfast rooms in vaulted cellars, or then again the high ceilings and wrought-iron balconies of the classic Haussmannian terrace, provide charm and an authenticity that can make up for any lack of space or services. There has recently been an influx of international luxury hotel groups, and even many of the small hotels have been renovated over the past few years bringing them up to scratch with quality beds, air conditioning and stylish decor.

France is in the process of updating its ratings system, replacing the old 0 to 4 star luxe categories by 1 to 5 stars, which means that the two systems currently coexist. Although there are some 2,000 hotels and nearly 75,000 hotel rooms, the city gets heavily booked up during the fashion shows, the interior decoration fair or events like the biennial motor show. The period when the city is quietest and hotel rates are lowest is in August.

**HOTEL PRICES**
Prices for an average double room in high season not including breakfast

€€€€ over €500
€€€ €250–500
€€ €150–250
€ under €150

# Luxury Without Limits

### Le Meurice
⬛ **Louvre**
228 rue de Rivoli; tel: 01 44 58 10 10;
www.lemeurice.com; map C3; €€€€

Splendidly positioned opposite
the Tuileries, Le Meurice has been
receiving guests in suitably regal
style since 1835 but has also known
how to update. The 160 rooms and
suites present a sea of pastel satins
to the eye. Reception rooms sparkle
with chandeliers, yet have been
subtly revisited by Philippe Starck,
with surreal furnishings in the Dali
lounge. There's an elegant spa,
superb restaurant (p.50) and the
staff are able to lay on anything from
treasure hunts for children through
to meals for pets.

### Shangri-La Paris
█ Champs-Elysées
10 avenue d'Iéna; tel: 01 53 67 19 98;
www.shangri-la.com; map C2; €€€€
The Hong Kong group's grand arrival
in France combines Asian calm and a
couldn't-be-more French style in the
mansion erected by Prince Roland
Bonaparte – explorer, botanist,
ethnologist and great-nephew of
Napoleon. Original salons are laden
in gilding and imperial motifs.
Bedrooms come in sybaritic Empire
style, and some have astonishing
views of the Eiffel Tower. There are
three restaurants and a bar where
you can try the Pink Lady cocktail,
named after eccentric former tenant
Lady Wendel.

### Le Royal Monceau Raffles Paris
█ Monceau
37 avenue Hoche; tel: 01 42 99 88 00;
www.leroyalmonceau.com; map E5; €€€€
The Royal Monceau Raffles Paris
has been reborn in the expert hands
of Philippe Starck as an artistic
hotel for the creative (and rich). The
ground floor is a brilliantly buzzy
crossroads between salons and Bar
Long, La Cuisine and Il Carpaccio
restaurants, an art bookshop and art
gallery – on top of the photographic
collection disseminated throughout
the guest rooms – concept store
and bright red *fumoir* (cigar bar).
There's an in-house cinema, an art
concierge, and a guitar amid the
creative clutter in every one of the 85
rooms and 61 suites.

# Boudoir Beauties

### Hôtel du Petit Moulin
#### Marais
29-31 rue de Poitou; tel: 01 42 74 10 10;
www.hoteldupetitmoulin.com; map D5; €€€

An old bakery in the Marais has been
transformed by Christian Lacroix
into one of the most romantic small
hotels in Paris. This is a chic insider
address where the 17 rooms each evoke
a different mood or voyage using
luscious fabrics and daring colour
combinations, and with a casual pop-
hued bar in the old bistro downstairs.

### Relais Christine
#### St-Germain
3 rue Christine; tel: 01 40 51 60 80;
www.relais-christine.com; map C4; €€€

There's a definite whiff of a bygone
aristocratic age in this lovely St-
Germain mansion, with its paved
entrance courtyard and panelled
drawing room. The 51 rooms vary from
minimalist chic to florals. Breakfast is
served in vaulted cellars – the remains
of a 13th-century monastery – where
there's also an elegant spa and a gym.

### Hôtel de l'Athénée
#### Opéra
19 rue Caumartin; tel: 01 40 17 99 29;
www.hotel-athenee.com; map C5; €€€

This snug 20-room hideaway has been
decorated in suitably operatic style by
Jacques Garcia as a plush tribute to
the nearby Palais Garnier. The intimate
bedrooms are themed according to
*La Traviata*, *Don Giovanni*, *Aida* and
*Faust*, and there's a sultry, boudoir-like
bar, where you sit on velvet chairs,
watched by photos of operatic divas.

### Hôtel des Grands-Hommes
#### Latin Quarter
17 place du Panthéon; tel: 01 46 34 19
60; www.hoteldesgrandshommes.com;
map D3; €€€

A dignified 18th-century hotel which
has been beautifully redone in
neoclassical hommage to the great men
of France reposing in the Panthéon.
The 31 rooms are intense cocoons of
classical wallpaper and portrait busts.
Many overlook the Panthéon; the best
have small balconies and views.

# Designer Style

### Pershing Hall
**Champs-Elysées**
49 rue Pierre-Charron; tel: 01 58 36 58 00;
www.pershinghall.com; map E3; €€€€
Set in the 19th-century mansion that
served as US General Pershing's World
War I HQ (spot the flame of liberty in
the ironwork), this is a small luxury
hotel with the aura of a grand one. The
26 rooms and suites are calm havens of
brown, cream and natural oak; but the
showstopper has to be botanist Patrick
Blanc's lushly planted vertical garden.

### Mama Shelter
**Beyond the Centre/Charonne**
109 rue de Bagnolet; tel: 01 43 48 48 48;
www.mamashelter.com; map F2; €
Streetwise urban design from Philippe
Starck in an out-of-the-way district has
made this one of the hottest addresses
in town, with a buzzy restaurant and
cocktail bar. Bedrooms mix exposed
concrete and graphic carpets with
fairground masks that double as
lampshades and all are equipped with
multimedia i-Mac and microwave.

### Seven Hôtel
**Latin Quarter**
20 rue Berthollet; tel: 01 43 31 47 52;
www.sevenhotelparis.com; map D1; €€€
Modern design is often deadpan
cool, the Seven (*also pictured p.169*)
is offbeat and fun with seven themed
suites, each crazier than the last: James
Bond, Alice in Wonderland, cave-man
seduction... The 'standard' rooms
haven't been forgotten though, with
intriguing levitating beds. There's a
bubbly velvet bar and breakfast is great.

### Hôtel Design de la Sorbonne
**Latin Quarter**
6 rue Victor-Cousin; tel: 01 43 54 58 08;
www.hotelsorbonne.com; map C3; €€€
This old Latin Quarter address has had
an invigorating designer makeover, in
a neo-baroque feast of acid pinks and
greens and clashing turquoise and
chocolate, with new bathrooms and
an i-Mac in every room. Only the attic
has kept its original brass bed, making
a romantic statement, with claw-foot
bath and Parisian rooftop views.

# Family-Friendly

### Jeanne d'Arc
🔲 **Marais**
3 rue de Jarente; tel: 01 48 87 62 11;
www.hoteljeannedarc.com; map D4; €
A gaudy, Gaudi-esque art nouveau
mirror in the breakfast room and
artworks around the corridors set
the tone at this characterful hotel,
which has friendly staff and a relaxed
atmosphere. Rooms are bigger than
usual for a budget hotel, with the
several that can sleep three or four
being ideal for families. Most rooms
have recently been attractively
redone, ditching old-fashioned
florals in favour of taffeta curtains,
colour-washed walls and sleek new
bathrooms.

### Hôtel Bel-Ami
🔲 **St-Germain**
7-11 rue St-Benoît; tel: 01 42 61 53 53;
www.hotel-bel-ami.com; map B5; €€€
This stylish St-Germain hotel is
very popular with the British and
Japanese fashion sets but is also a
place that gives a genuine welcome
to children. Special family packages
are available, with kids' bathrobes,
colouring sets and Playstations, and
it's possible to either add an extra
bed or have interconnecting rooms.
Rooms are stylish and contemporary
in spice colours; some have large
windows from the building's days as a
printworks, while a few have views of
Eglise St-Germain-des-Prés.

# Village Paris

## Hôtel de Lutèce
### Islands & Marais
65 rue St-Louis-en-l'Ile; tel: 01 43 26 23 52;
www.paris-hotel-lutece.com; map C3; €€
It's village life right in the heart of Paris
at this hotel on the high street of the
Ile St-Louis. Downstairs preserves the
island's Louis XIII atmosphere with
antique furniture, period panelling, old
*tomettes* (terracotta tiles) and a lovely
stone fireplace. Bedrooms are attractive
with beamed ceilings and sparkling
new bathrooms.

## Hôtel des Grandes-Ecoles
### Latin Quarter
75 rue du Cardinal-Lemoine; tel: 01 43 26 79
23; www.hotel-grandes-ecoles.com; map D3; €
This hotel is one of those surprises
you suddenly come across in Paris: a
tranquil pale pink stucco house hidden
down a cobbled lane, just seconds
from the hubbub of the Contrescarpe.
Opened in the 1920s as a B&B for
visiting academics, the 51 bedrooms
are charmingly rustic, though regularly
redone. But the true treat is the garden.

## Le Relais Montmartre
### Montmartre
6 rue Constance, tel: 01 42 61 53 53; www.
relaismontmartre.fr; map D4; €€
Lots of loving care has been put into
this charming little hotel halfway up
the *butte*, near the bars and foodshops
of Abbesses, whose ground floor feels
like a welcoming private home. The
26 bedrooms are decorated in pretty
florals but what you immediately notice
are the beams, each room's painted in a
different colour – fuschia, lilac, mauve.

## Citizen Hôtel
### Belleville
96 quai de Jemmapes; tel: 01 83 62 55 50;
http://lecitizenhotel.com; map A6; €€
This is a relaxed new hotel on the
banks of the burgeoning Canal St-
Martin. The 12 rooms are pared back
yet beautifully crafted to maximise
space. Several have lovely window seats
giving a grandstand view of the Canal;
a couple with two bedrooms are ideal
for families. Downstairs, Usagi is a very
zen Japanese bento box restaurant.

# Affordable Chic

### Hôtel des Bons Enfants
**Louvre**

3-5 rue des Bons-Enfants; tel: 01 42 61 47 31; www.hotellouvrebonsenfants.com; map E2; €€

Bohemian modern meets Baroque in this small hotel, set within the confines of a 16th-century building tagged onto Palais-Royal and with a friendly vibe and cheerfully quirky decor. The 23 colourful rooms have comfortable beds and modern bathrooms, a couple have four posters; those overlooking the street are better than those on a minuscule courtyard. There's a small fitness room and a colourful lounge with mirrors, red sofas and a computer for guests' use.

### Hôtel Amour
**Pigalle**

8 rue de Navarin; tel: 01 48 78 31 80; www.hotelamourparis.fr; map E3; €€

In trendy SoPi (south Pigalle), the Hôtel Amour signalled a new breed of artists' hotel: a deliberately low-tech, 'undesign' establishment, low on services yet high on cool. The brainchild of graffiti artist-cum-nightclub entrepreneur André and Thierry Costes, some of the 20 rooms were created by artists – André, Pierre Le Tan, M/M (Paris) – while others have artfully chosen flea market finds and loud Marimekko print curtains. Downstairs there's a laidback restaurant, with outdoor tables in the overgrown courtyard.

### Hôtel du Champ de Mars
🔲 Invalides
7 rue du Champ de Mars; tel: 01 45 51 52 30; www.hotelduchampdemars.com; map B6; €

A pristine floral cocoon, the Champ de Mars provides boutique charm at low prices in a smart residential district, with the food shops of rue Cler around the corner and the Eiffel Tower at the end of the street. There's a romantic boudoir-style lobby and 25 bedrooms decked out in floral *toile de jouy* fabrics, in sunny yellow or cornflower blue.

### Hôtel Arvor St-Georges
🔲 Pigalle
8 rue Laferrière, 9th; tel: 01 48 78 60 92; www.arvor-hotel-paris.com; €€

This tastefully *bobo* (bourgeois bohème) hideaway, located on a quiet crescent, succeeds in being both refreshingly simple – lots of white, accent colours, furniture from fleamarkets – and feel calmly cultivated, with art posters and original photos on the walls, paperback novels and art books to browse.

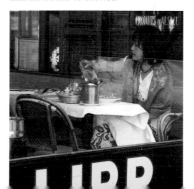

### Hôtel Michelet Odéon
🔲 St-Germain
6 place de l'Odéon; tel: 01 53 10 05 60; www.hotelmicheletodeon.com; map B3; €

Located in an 18th-century building on the beautiful square facing the historic Odéon theatre, and just near the Luxembourg gardens, this long-standing budget address is proof that you can find bargains even in the very best *quartiers*. The bedrooms have been stylishly redecorated in suave brown tones and natural wood bedheads and desks.

# Going Green

### Solar Hôtel
■ **Montparnasse**
22 rue Boulard, tel: 01 43 21 08 20;
www.solarhotel.fr; map E1; €

While many hotels pay lip service to going green, the 'ecological, economical and activist' Solar Hôtel has done so to an impressive degree and at bargain prices – able to lay claim to energy and water saving, waste sorting, locally sourced organic breakfasts and bikes for guests to borrow. The blue-painted rooms are practical and no frills and you're encouraged to use the stairs rather than the lift but the mood is sociable nonetheless, and there's a shady wood-decked garden where you can picnic.

### Best Western Premier Hôtel Regent's Garden
■ **Monceau**
6 rue Pierre-Demours; tel: 01 45 74 07 30;
www.hotel-regents-paris.com; map C5; €€€

A recent refurbishment at the Regent's Garden has jazzed up the rooms and achieved the European Ecolabel, however the stately villa built by Napoleon III for his personal physician still retains a cosseted, private-house feel. Many of the guests are regulars who greet the staff by name, rooms are in the classic mould but not overly so, and there's a lovely, vaguely Oriental garden into which you can wander out for breakfast (organic and fairtrade).

# Historic Visions

### Hôtel Lancaster
■ Champs-Elysées
7 rue de Berri; tel: 01 40 76 40 76;
www.hotel-lancaster.fr; map E4; €€€€
The hotel where Marlene Dietrich hid out for three years in the 1930s is an intimate period retreat. Her vast suite has been preserved, and the other rooms, filled with antiques, ormolu clocks and oil paintings are pretty good too. The superb Table du Lancaster serves Michel Troisgros' light modern cooking in a plush lounge setting.

### Hôtel d'Aubusson
■ St-Germain
33 rue Dauphine; tel: 01 43 29 43 43;
www.hoteldaubusson.com; map C5; €€€
This 17th-century *hôtel particulier* on an animated St-Germain street has kept all its historic aura with its lofty carriageway entrance, flagstoned reception hall and a drawing room hung with Aubussson tapestries. The 49 bedrooms are high-ceilinged and romantic, some with beams and four-poster beds.

### Saint James Paris
■ Champs-Elysées
43 avenue Bugeaud; tel: +33 1 44 05 81 81;
www.saint-james-paris.com; map A4; €€€
Staying at the Saint-James is a bit like being invited to a slightly crazy country house party. Built in French château style to accommodate impoverished scholars, it has recently been redecorated in a glorious mix of Empire, chinoiserie and Scottish manse, with fake parquet carpet and an optical illusion staircase.

### Hôtel Caron de Beaumarchais
■ Marais
12 rue Vieille-du-Temple; tel: 01 42 72 34 12;
www.carondebeaumarchais.com; map C4; €€
Walking into this hotel is like stepping into an 18th-century stage set: a shrine to the playwright Beaumarchais, author of the then-radical *The Marriage of Figaro*. The 19 pretty bedrooms are compact and deliciously romantic with exposed beams, antique desks, sprigged curtains and chandeliers, but with 21st-century amenities too.

### Hôtel d'Angleterre
■ St-Germain
44 rue Jacob; tel: 01 42 60 34 72;
www.hotel-dangleterre.com; map B5; €€
L'Angleterre stands out: today as a calm, well-bred refuge, yesterday as the British embassy, where the Treaty of Paris recognising American independence was drafted in 1783. Later, Hemingway slept in room 14. The staircase is listed; many of the 27 rooms have fireplaces and antiques, a couple colossal stripey marble bathrooms.

# Essentials

## A

### Arrival

*By Air*

**Arriving from Paris Charles de Gaulle**
Most international flights arrive at
**Paris Charles de Gaulle airport** (www.
aeroportsdeparis.fr), 27km (17 miles)
north of the city.

The most reliable and inexpensive
way into town is by **RER line B**, which
takes around 45 minutes to Châtelet-
Les Halles (€9.10). There are two
stations: Aéroport Charles de Gaulle
1 serves Terminals 1 and 3; Aéroport
Charles de Gaulle 2/TGV serves
Terminal 2 and is also a mainline
station for high-speed trains all over
France. The free, driverless CDGVAL
light railway connects the different
terminals, RER stations and car parks.

There are also assorted bus services,
including the **Roissybus** to Opéra (€10)
and **Air France** coaches to Etoile/Porte
Maillot and Montparnasse (€15–16.50).

Count on at least €50–60 for a
taxi into town, plus supplements for
each piece of luggage. **Paris Airport
Shuttle** (www.paris-airport-shuttle.
com), **Paris Shuttle** (www.parishuttle.
com) and **Airport Connection** (www.
airport-connection.com) run minibus
services between the airport and hotels
(€20–27). Allow plenty of time if you're
planning to return by taxi or minibus.

**Arriving from Paris Orly**
A few flights arrive at the smaller **Orly
airport** (www.aeroportsdeparis.fr),

14km (9 miles) south of the city centre.
To reach Paris, take the Orlybus (€6.90)
to Denfert-Rochereau station in Paris,
every 15–20 minutes 6am–11.30pm. The
costlier Orlyval automatic train (€8.30)
is a shuttle to Antony (the nearest RER
to Orly). It runs every 4–7 minutes,
6am–11pm, and takes 35 minutes. Allow
around €30 for a taxi.

*By Train*
**Eurostar** (UK tel: 08432-186 186; www.
eurostar.com; France tel: 3635; www.
voyages-sncf.fr) runs fast, frequent rail
services from London (St Pancras) or
Ashford station to Paris Gare du Nord.
The service runs about 12 times a day
and takes around 2 hours 15 mins.

*By Car*
There are frequent car ferries between
Dover and Calais run by **SeaFrance**
(UK tel: 0845 458 0666/France tel: 03
21 17 70 26; www.seafrance.com) and
**P&O Ferries** (UK tel: 08716 645 645/
France tel: 0825 120 156; www.poferries.
com) or you can take **Le Shuttle** (UK
tel: 08443-353 535/France tel: 08
10 63 03 04; www.eurotunnel.com)
through the Channel Tunnel between
Folkestone and Calais. It is 290km (180
miles) between Calais and Paris.

*By Coach*
National Express Eurolines (tel: 08717-
818178; www.nationalexpress.com)
runs services daily from London's
Victoria Coach Station to Paris Gare
Routière Galliéni, 28 avenue du

Général de Gaulle, Bagnolet (tel: 08 92 89 90 91; www.eurolines.fr.), taking six to eight hours.

# C

## Climate

The average maximum in July and August is 25°C (77°F), the average minimum 15°C (59°F), but 27°C (81°F) is not unusual. In January, expect a maximum of 6°C (43°F) and a minimum of 1°C (34°F). Snow is rare, but it can rain all year round, so bring an umbrella.

## Crime and Safety

In the event of theft, a report must be made in person at the nearest police station (*commissariat*) as soon as possible. See www.prefecture-police-paris.interieur.gouv.fr for addresses of stations; for emergency help tel: 17.

If you lose your passport, report it to your consulate after notifying the police.

**Security:** It is advisable to take the same precautions in Paris as you would in any other major city, notably watching out for pickpockets on public transport and shielding your PIN at ATM machines. Known centres of prostitution (such as parts of the Bois de Boulogne) are best avoided at night.

# D

## Disabled Travellers

The Disabled People Access section on the Paris tourist board website (www.parisinfo.com) has information on transport, equipment and services for the physically, mentally, sight or hearing disabled. It indicates where there is disabled access to sights, museums, hotels and restaurants, including the new national Tourisme et Handicaps labelling scheme (www.tourisme-handicap.org).

**UK Organisations:** RADAR, the Royal Association for Disability and Rehabilitation, 12 City Forum, 250 City Road, London EC1V 8AF; tel: 020-7250 3222; www.radar.org.uk.

**US Organisations:** Society for Accessible Travel and Hospitality (SATH), 347 Fifth Avenue, Suite 605, New York, NY 10016; tel: 212-447 7284; www.sath.org.

## Driving

You probably won't want to drive in central Paris, which is well covered by public transport (*see below*), but it can be useful for outer districts or suburbs. To drive in France, you must be at least 18. If you are bringing your own car, very few hotels have their own car parks, but they may offer special rates for a nearby car park.

To hire a car you will need to show your driving licence (held for at least a year) and passport. You will also need a major credit card, or a large deposit. The minimum age for renting cars is 21, although a young driver's supplement is usually payable for those under 25. Third-party insurance is compulsory, and full cover is recommended.

The major car hire companies all have branches at the main mainline stations and airports, including Avis (tel: 08 21 23 07 60; www.avis.fr/ UK tel: 08445 810 147; www.avis.co.uk), Europcar (tel: 08 25 35 83 58; www.europcar.fr; UK tel: 08713 308 1087) and Hertz (tel: 01 39 38 38 38; www.hertz.fr; UK tel: 08708 448 844).

# E

## Electricity
220-volt, 50-cycle AC is universal, generally with a three-pin plug, or with two-pin plugs for smaller appliances. British visitors should buy an adaptor (*adaptateur*); American visitors will need a transformer (*transformateur*).

## Embassies and Consulates
**Australia:** Embassy: 4 rue Jean-Rey, 15th; tel: 01 40 59 33 00.
**Canada:** Embassy: 35 avenue Montaigne, 8th; tel: 01 44 43 29 00.
**Republic of Ireland:** Embassy: 12 avenue Foch, 16th; tel: 01 44 17 67 00, embassyofireland.fr.
**UK:** Consulate: 16 rue d'Anjou, 8th; tel: 01 44 51 31 00; http://ukinfrance.fco.gov.uk/en.
**US:** Embassy: Consular Section, 4 avenue Gabriel, 1st; tel: 01 43 12 22 22; http://france.usembassy.gov.

## Emergency numbers
Ambulance (SAMU): tel: 15
Fire brigade (pompiers): tel: 18

Police (police secours): tel: 17
All, from a mobile phone: tel: 112

# G

## Gay and Lesbian
Paris is generally gay-friendly, with the most visible gay community located in the Marais. The Centre Lesbien Gay Bi & Trans (63 rue Beaubourg, 3rd; tel: 01 43 57 21 47; www.centrelgbtparis.org) provides information and support and is an umbrella organisation for gay associations.

# H

## Health
EU Nationals are eligible for medical treatment under the French health service. You will have to pay for the treatment, but are entitled to claim back up to 70 percent if you have a European Health Insurance Card (www.ehic.org.uk).

Non-EU visitors should take out health insurance.

The private American Hospital (Hôpital Américain de Paris, 63 boulevard Victor Hugo, Neuilly-sur-Seine; tel: 01 46 41 25 25; www.american-hospital.org) has a casualty service with bilingual staff.

*Pharmacies*
Most pharmacies open Monday to Saturday 9 or 10am to 7 or 8pm. On Sunday, they post the addresses of the nearest Sunday-opening pharmacies in their windows. A 24-hour pharmacy

is Pharmacie Dhéry, 84 avenue des Champs-Elysées; tel: 01 45 62 02 41.

# I
## Internet
Most hotels have Wi-fi access, which is usually free – check at the reception desk first. There is also free Wi-fi in municipal parks and in train stations, as well as at some cafés.

24-hour internet café **Milk** (www.milkclub.com) has six branches in Paris, including 13 rue Soufflot in the Latin Quarter and 28 rue du Quatre Septembre near Opéra.

# L
## Lost Property
To reclaim lost items in Paris, go in person (with ID) to the Bureau des Objets Trouvés, 36 rue des Morillons, 15th; tel: 08 21 00 25 25; Mon–Thur 8.30am–5pm, Fri 8.30am–4.30pm; metro: Convention.

# M
## Maps
Most hotels can provide a basic foldout map, but if you really want to explore, it's worth investing in a small mapbook – such as *Paris pratique par arrondissement*, published by L'Indispensable, which covers the 20 *arrondissements*, or the larger *Maxi Paris*, which includes the inner suburbs. *Fleximap Paris*, published by Insight Guides, is a laminated fold-out map. Ask in metro stations for a map of the metro and bus routes.

## Money
**Currency.** France uses the euro, divided into 100 centimes. Coins (*pièces*) come in one, two, five, 10, 20 and 50 *centimes*, and one and two euros. Banknotes (*billets*) come in five, 10, 20, 50, 100, 200 and 500 euros, but note that shops are often unwilling to accept the largest denomination notes.

**Cash Machines.** The easiest way to take out money is to use an ATM, with a debit or credit card such as Visa, MasterCard, Maestro or Cirrus, etc, and your PIN. Note that travellers' cheques are rarely used.

**Credit Cards.** Most shops, restaurants and hotels accept credit cards, especially Visa and MasterCard; there may be a minimum sum of 10 or 15 euros.

## Museums and Monuments
The permanent collections are free at Paris's municipal museums, including the Petit Palais, Musée Carnavalet, Musée d'Art Moderne de la Ville de Paris, Musée Cernuschi and the Maison de Victor Hugo, though you usually have to pay for temporary exhibitions.

Permanent collections at national museums, including the Louvre, Musée d'Orsay, Centre Pompidou, Musée Rodin, and national monuments, such as the Arc de Triomphe and Sainte Chapelle, are free for all EU residents/nationals aged under 26 (bring passport), for non-EU nationals under 18 if accompanied by an adult, and for everybody on the first Sunday of the month. Full admission prices usually vary between €6 and €10.

For independently owned museums, tarifs vary but are generally free for children under 12 or under 18.

If you are planning on some intensive museum-visiting, it may be worth investing in the Carte Paris Musées museum pass – which costs €35 for two days, €50 for four days and €65 for six days.

Most museums close on either Monday or Tuesday. Check before you go.

# N
## Newspapers and Magazines
The main daily newspapers are centre-left *Le Monde*, more conservative *Le Figaro* – which includes the *Figaroscope* listings supplement on Wednesdays – and left-slanted *Libération*. Less highbrow *Le Parisien* has a large section devoted to local news, the *Journal du Dimanche* is the main Sunday paper. Free newspapers distributed in or outside Métro stations include *Metro* and *Direct Matin*. Weekly news magazines include *Le Point*, *L'Express*, *Nouvel Observateur*, and more recent arrival *Marianne*. There are a vast number of consumer magazines but everyone likes to keep an eye on who's featured in *Paris Match*.

The British press is also widely available, as is *USA Today* and the Paris-based *International Herald Tribune*.

# P
## Post and Stamps
Post Offices: Most branches open Mon–Fri 8am-7 or 8pm, Sat 8am-noon, sometimes with reduced hours in August. The central post office at 52 rue du Louvre, 1st, is open all night (Mon–Sat 7.30am-6am, Sun 10am-midnight); www.laposte.fr. However, unless you are sending a parcel or registered post, it is usually easier to buy stamps (*timbres*) at a tobacconist (*tabac*).

## Public Holidays (jours fériés)
Banks, public buildings, and many museums and shops close on public holidays, during which transport runs on Sunday schedules.
**1 Jan** Nouvel An – New Year's Day
**Mar/Apr** Lundi de Pâques – Easter Monday
**1 May** Fête du Travail – Labour Day
**8 May** Fête de la Victoire – VE Day
**Mid/late May** Ascension – Ascension
**Late May/early June** Lundi de Pentecôte – Whit Monday
**14 July** Le Quartorze Juillet – Bastille Day
**15 Aug** Fête de l'Assomption – Assumption
**1 Nov** Toussaint – All Saints' Day
**11 Nov** Le Onze Novembre – Armistice Day, 1918
**25 Dec** Noël – Christmas

## Public Transport

A generally efficient public transport system is run by the RATP (tel: 3246; www.ratp.fr), incorporating the metro, RER suburban express, buses and tramway.

*Metro and RER*

The metro has 14 lines. Services run from 5.30am to 12.30am, extended until around 1am on Friday and Saturday nights, with metros every two or three minutes at peak hours and more limited services on Sunday and bank holidays. The five **RER suburban express** lines go from central Paris far into the Ile-de-France suburbs, including the RER B to Aéroport Charles de Gaulle and the Stade de France. Within the city centre it can be useful for speedy journeys: for example Châtelet-Les Halles to Charles de Gaulle-Etoile is only two stops on the RER and seven stops by metro.

*Buses and Trams*

Some 50 bus routes criss-cross the city. It is a good way to see the city at ground level – and also a relatively efficient one, as sections of many routes now run in bus lanes. Some routes stop at around 9pm and not all routes run on Sunday.

In Montmartre, you can also take the Montmartrobus, capable of navigating the narrow streets of the *butte*, and the Funicular, which climbs up the side of square Willette to Sacré-Coeur. Both take standard RATP tickets or passes.

**Night buses.** 47 Noctilien night bus routes run – at rather long intervals – between central Paris and the suburbs from 12.30am to 5.30am, operating from five principal hubs at Châtelet, Gare St-Lazare, Gare Montparnasse, Gare de l'Est and Gare de Lyon.

**The tram.** Paris has three modern tramlines. Only line 3, which runs along the boulevards des Maréchaux on the Left Bank between Pont du Garigliano and Porte d'Ivry is in Paris itself (currently being extended north of the river). Line 1 serves Seine St-Denis in the northeast suburbs, line 2 runs along the Seine in the western suburbs.

*Tickets*

The standard ticket (€1.70), designated t+, is valid on buses, metro and tramways, plus the RER within central Paris (zone 1). It allows changes on the metro network or between metro and RER or one change of bus or bus/tram within a period of 90 minutes (but not changes between metro and bus). It is usually simpler and more economical to buy a *carnet* of ten tickets (€12.50). Tickets should be validated when you get onto the bus or go through the metro barrier. Keep your ticket in case of spot inspections and to get out of RER stations. Separate tickets have to be bought for RER stations outside of the central zone and for airport buses.

If you are planning to use the bus or metro a lot, or to take the RER into the suburbs, another option is a one-day **Mobilis** ticket, priced according to number of zones. The **Paris Visite** pass, valid one, two, three, or five days, is aimed at tourists and covers either zones 1-3 or zones 1-6 (not including airports). It includes discounts on certain tourist attractions, although it often works out more expensive than a carnet or Mobilis pass.

**Navigo.** If you're staying for longer time and are intending to use public transport regularly, you may want to buy a Navigo pass: a magnetic travelcard (photo required) available by the calendar month or weekly (valid Mon–Sun). Navigo Passe is for residents of Paris and the Ile-de-France, the **Navigo Découverte** is available to anyone for an initial €5 plus the subscription.

Individual tickets, *carnets* and Navigo recharges can all be bought with cash or credit cards at ticket machines or ticket offices inside metro stations; *carnets* are available from some tobacconists too. Single-use tickets (€1.80) can also be bought from bus drivers but do not allow changes.

*Vélib*
Vélib (www.velib.paris.fr) is the enormously successful municipal bike hire scheme, with over 20,000 bikes and some 1,500 ranks in Paris and the inner suburbs. One- or seven-day subscriptions (€1/€5) can be taken out on the spot with a credit card. The first 30 minutes of each journey are free, it's €1 for the next 30 minutes and the rates rise sharply thereafter. There are a growing number of cycle lanes but note that while some are dedicated others are perilously shared with buses and taxis.

*Taxis*
Taxis can be hailed in the street or at taxi ranks, although are often in short supply as they tend to congregate at the airports and mainline stations. On old taxis, a white light on the roof indicates when it is free; a new more visible system is being introduced with a green light to indicate when the taxi is free and red when it is occupied. Rates differ according to the zones covered and time of day (there are higher rates between 5pm and 7am and on Sunday), and extra charges for luggage and for pick-up at a station or airport. Taxi drivers usually won't take more than three passengers. The fourth, if admitted, pays a supplement.

Central call centre 01 45 30 30 30; G7 taxis switchboard in English 01 41 27 66 99.

# R

## Restaurants

Restaurants generally serve from around noon to around 2.30pm and from 7.30 or 8pm to around 10.30pm. If you want to eat outside these hours, your best bet is probably a café or brasserie, which often serve food all day and stay open until late. Cafés generally open at around 8am or 9am to serve breakfast. Many restaurants close on Monday and Sunday, and for all or part of August.

A service charge of 12-15% is always

included in restaurant bills; any additional tip is purely optional, and bread and tap water are free. As well as à la carte dishes, many restaurants have good value menus at lunch time, and bistros often have a *menu-carte* system offering two or three courses for a fixed price.

# S

## Smoking
Smoking is banned in all public buildings including stations, airports, museums, shops and offices, restaurants, bars and the public areas of hotels. Smoking is permitted in hotel bedrooms, unless designated non-smoking rooms, and on outdoor terraces at cafés and restaurants, or if they have a specially closed and ventilated *fumoir* (smoking room).

# T

## Telephones
All telephone numbers in France have 10 digits. Paris and Ile-de-France numbers begin with 01. 06 numbers are for mobile phones. Numbers beginning 08 range from 0800 freephone numbers to premium rate calls. For the operator, call 12.

Directory enquiries are available from various providers, including 118000, 118008 and 118218 or use www.pagesjaune.fr.
**Calling from Abroad.** To dial Paris from abroad dial 00, followed by 33, the country code for France, followed by

the Paris number, leaving off the 0 at the start. To call other countries from France, dial 00, then the country code: Australia 61, UK 44, US and Canada 1.
**Public Telephone Boxes.** Most phone boxes in Paris are operated with a card (*télécarte*), bought from tobacconists, newsstands and post offices; some also take credit/debit cards.

## Time Zones
France is one hour ahead of Greenwich Mean Time (GMT) and six ahead of Eastern Standard Time.

## Tourist Information
Paris Convention and Visitors Bureau (25 rue des Pyramides, 1st; tel: 08 92 68 30 00; http://en.parisinfo.com; daily 9am–7pm). There are branches at Gare du Nord and Anvers (72 boulevard Rochechouart) open daily; Gare de l'Est and Gare de Lyon open Mon–Sat; Porte de Versailles open during trade fairs; plus summer information stands at Champs-Elysées-Clémenceau, Bastille, Hôtel de Ville and Notre-Dame.

# V

## Visas
All visitors to France require a valid passport. EU nationals do not need visas, nor do most visitors from the US, Australia, Canada and New Zealand if staying for less than 90 days. Nationals of other countries may need a visa; if in doubt, check with the French Consulate in your home country, or see www.diplomatie.gouv.fr.

# Index

---

**Insight Select Guide: Paris**
**Written by:** Natasha Edwards
**Edited by:** Alexia Georgiou
**Layout by:** Ian Spick
**Maps:** Apa Cartography Department
**Picture Manager:** Steven Lawrence
**Series Editor:** Carine Tracanelli

**Photography:** Alamy 29, 35, 43, 61, 70, 73, 87, 88, 89, 95, 105, 129, 137, 153, 154, 160, 167,176B; Hotels Athnee/Jaques Garcia 172B; Chantal Carousel 39; Citizen Hotel 175; Colette 53; APA Kevin Cummins 4/5, 6, 8T, 11, 12, 14T, 15, 17, 22, 54, 58, 62, 64, 75, 80, 84, 85, 90, 92, 94, 96, 103, 106, 109, 116, 123, 135, 141, 148, 157, 158, 163, 176T, 177/T, 178; Alexander Duret-Lutz 93; Vincent Fillion 42; Fotolia 146; Galerie Matthieu Richard 124; Getty Images 57, 77, 100; F.G Grandin/MNHN 10; APA Ilpo Musto 3B/T, 7, 8B, 9, 12T, 13, 14B, 16/T, 19, 26, 28, 30, 31, 32, 33, 34, 37, 38, 44, 48, 51, 56, 68/69, 91, 110, 115, 118, 125, 127, 130, 134, 138, 161; Istockphoto 27, 55, 60, 76, 107, 136, 145; Jeanne D'Arc 174Petit Moulin 41; APA Sylvaine Poitau 142; Hotel Lancaster 179; Langladure 147; Lasserre 70; Stephen Lea 117; Le Grand Vefour 49; Le Meurice 50, 170/T; Mathieu Lecarme 78; Levitation/Serge Ramelli 173B; LPLT 122; Royal Monceau 171B; Marmottan Monet 152; Mandarin Oriental 79; David Moniaux 120; Musee Jaquemart 72; Palais de Tokyo 74; Parisette 159; Patrick Giraud 162; Courtesy Penguin 121; Pershing Hall 173; Hotel du Petit Moulin 172T; Aaron Perkins 119; Photolibrary 2T, 128, 140, 164, 165; Popolon 101; Rex Features 52, 143; RMN Franck Raux 86; Seven Hotels 168/169; Shangrila 171T; Topfoto 142; APA Ming Tang Evans 63; Jean-Louis Vandevivère 104.

**Basemap data:** on pp.150-1 derived from Open-StreetMap © OpenStreetMap and Contributors, CC-BY-SA

**First Edition 2012**
© 2012 Apa Publications UK Ltd.
Printed in Germany

*Distributed in the UK and Ireland by:*
Dorling Kindersley Ltd,
a Penguin Group company, 80 Strand, London,
WC2R 0RL, UK;
email: customerservice@dk.com

*Distributed in the United States by:*
Ingram Publisher Services
1 Ingram Boulevard, PO Box 3006,
La Vergne, TN 37086-1986, USA;
email: customer.service@ingrampublisher services.com

*Distributed in Australia by:*
Universal Publishers
PO Box 307, St Leonards NSW 1590,
Australia;
email: sales@universalpublishers.com.au

*Worldwide distribution by:*
APA Publications GmbH & Co. Verlag KG
(Singapore branch)
7030 Ang Mo Kio Ave 5, 08-65 Northstar @ AMK,
Singapore 569880;
email: apasin@singnet.com.sg

Contacting the Editors
We would appreciate it if readers would alert us
to outdated information by writing to:
Apa Publications, PO Box 7910, London SE1
1WE, UK;
email: insight@apaguide.co.uk